Ayelet Waldman

Bad Mother

Ayelet Waldman is the author of *Daughter's Keeper*, *Love and Other Impossible Pursuits* and *Red Hook Road*. Her writing has appeared in *The New York Times*, *Salon*, *New York*, *Elle*, *Vogue*, and other publications. She and her husband, the novelist Michael Chabon, live in Berkeley, California, with their four children.

www.ayeletwaldman.com

Also by Ayelet Waldman

Love and Other Impossible Pursuits
Daughter's Keeper
Red Hook Road

Bad Mother

A Chronicle of Maternal Crimes, Minor Calamities,
and Occasional Moments of Grace

Ayelet Waldman

www.tworoadsbooks.com

First published in Great Britain in 2014 by Two Roads
An imprint of Hodder & Stoughton
An Hachette UK company

1

A CIP catalogue record for this title is available from the British Library

ISBN 978 1 444 76315 7

Printed and bound by CPI Group (UK) Ltd, Croydon CR0 4YY

Hodder & Stoughton policy is to use papers that are natural, renewable
and recyclable products and made from wood grown in sustainable forests.
The logging and manufacturing processes are expected to conform to the
environmental regulations of the country of origin.

Hodder & Stoughton Ltd
338 Euston Road
London NW1 3BH

To my sweet children,
Sophie, Ezekiel, Ida-Rose, and Abraham

Contents

Introduction:
Or, Life in Eighteen Pieces

The morning after my wedding, my husband, Michael, and I were lying on a vast expanse of white linen in the bridal suite of Berkeley's oldest hotel, engaging in a romantic tradition of newlyweds the world over: counting our loot. Sifting through the checks, I said, "What's with the multiples of eighteen? Fifty-four dollars, ninety. Wow, here's one for one eighty."

"Life," my new husband said.

"Life?"

"You know, *chai*. Didn't your grandmothers always give you checks in multiples of eighteen for your birthday?"

One of my grandmothers, I recalled, always sent a crisp five-dollar bill tucked into a birthday card. The other had presented me for most of the previous twenty-seven years with one of a series of Jewish-themed necklaces that, after the thirteenth or so, would go right into my underwear drawer, never to emerge again.

He explained, "It's *gematria*. The ancient Jewish system of numerical symbolism. Each Hebrew letter has a number value. You spell the Hebrew word for life, *chai*, with the letter *chet*, which equals eight, and the letter *yud*, which equals ten. *Chet, yud*, eight and ten. Eighteen stands for life."

Among the constellation of Stars of David twinkling in my underwear drawer lay tangled a number of gold and silver *chais*, necklaces bearing that two-letter word. One, with letters close to two inches high, had adorned the yoke of my forest green acrylic cowl-necked sweater in my eighth-grade yearbook picture; the silver was the precise shade of my braces. While I'd always known that *chai*, life, was a symbol of good luck, I had never been taught the significance of the number eighteen.

Since that morning fifteen years ago, I have received more checks in multiples of eighteen, as have my children on the occasions of their births and birthdays. Symbolic representations of life and luck, even if luck is understood to mean readily transferable into Spider-Man Legos, Polly Pockets, and handfuls of candy.

Once you have children, eighteen becomes a number with a certain magical weight. Eighteen is the age of majority. It's the age when they can vote (although not drink), when they graduate from high school and go off to college. Eighteen-year-olds are legally adults, I remember reminding my own mother when I was that age; you can't tell them what to do. And after your children turn eighteen, you are no longer responsible for them in the eyes of the law.

Except, of course, the law of the land is irrelevant; it's the law of your heart that matters. The law might think differently, but your children are yours forever, your responsibility until, at last, you are theirs.

This book is about the perils and joys of trying to be a decent mother in a world intent on making you feel like a bad one. Because it is about me, and my experience of motherhood, it is necessarily about the luckiest things that have ever happened to me—my four children and my husband—and thus it seems only fitting that I tell the story in eighteen chapters. It also seems fitting that I hesitate a moment before telling my story—our story—

to consider the question of whether it is appropriate to write about my children at all. Would a Good Mother keep her own counsel, button her lip? Does writing about my children make me a Bad Mother?

My children have given me their permission to write this book. I always share what I'm writing with them; I check in to make sure they're not uncomfortable and don't feel exposed. And there have been many times when I have decided, because of their trepidation or my own concern, not to tell a story or dwell on a topic. I am confident that I have not betrayed my children anywhere in these eighteen chapters. Still, they are under eighteen, and one of them can't even read. Their permission alone cannot justify the project.

The justification lies in the fact that the very writing of this book embodies my approach to motherhood, even, dare I say it, my philosophy. I believe that mothers should tell the truth, even—no, *especially*—when the truth is difficult. It's always easier, and in the short term can even feel right, to pretend everything is okay, and to encourage your children to do the same. But concealment leads to shame, and of all hurts shame is the most painful. Only if you name a problem, confront it head-on, drag it into the light, does it become surmountable. I always tell my kids that as soon as you have a secret, something about you that you are ashamed to have others find out, you have given other people the power to hurt you by exposing you.

One of the darkest, deepest shames so many of us mothers feel nowadays is our fear that we are Bad Mothers, that we are failing our children and falling far short of our own ideals. In these eighteen chapters I explore that fear. I turn over those rocks and expose the spidery places beneath. By presenting a faithful and honest record of my experience as a mother, I hope to show both my readers and my children how truth can redeem even what you fear might be the gravest of sins.

As I write this, Sophie is thirteen years old, Zeke just turned eleven, Rosie is seven, and Abraham, whom we most often call Abie, is just five. Thirty-six altogether. A multiple of eighteen.

My luck, my loves, my *chai*.

1. Bad Mother

I busted my first Bad Mother in the spring of 1994, on a Muni train in San Francisco. She was sitting on the edge of her seat, her young daughter standing between her knees. She had two barrettes clamped between her lips and a hair elastic stretched around the fingers of one hand. With her other hand she was brushing the little girl's long dark hair, trying to gather the slippery strands into a neat ponytail. It was not going well. She would smooth one side and then lose her grip on the other, or gather up the hair in the front only to watch the hairs at the nape of the girl's neck slide free. The ride was rough, the Muni car bucking and jerking along, causing the little girl periodically to lose her footing. When the driver took a turn too sharply, the little girl stumbled forward, her sudden motion causing her mother once again to lose hold of the ponytail. With a frustrated click of her tongue, the mother yanked a handful of the girl's hair, hard, and hissed, "Stand still!"

That's when, indignant, confident that someday, when it was my turn to brush my own daughter's hair, I would never be so abusive, I leaned forward in my seat, caught the woman's eye, and said, in a voice loud enough for everyone in the train car to hear, "Lady, we're all watching you."

We are always watching: the Bad Mother police force, in a perpetual state of alert-level orange. Sometimes the avatars of maternal evil that come to obsess us are grave and terrible, like Andrea

Yates, who was found not guilty by reason of insanity for drowning her five children in the bathtub. Sometimes our fixation on a particular Bad Mother has to do with our own racism, as in the national obsession in the 1980s with the mythical welfare queen, described by Ronald Reagan as a woman with "80 names, 30 addresses, [and] 12 Social Security cards," or the current hysteria about undocumented women giving birth to "anchor" babies in order to immunize themselves from deportation. Sometimes the crime is so lunatic that it approaches a kind of horrible grandeur, like that of Wendy Cook, a prostitute in Saratoga Springs who snorted cocaine off her baby's stomach while she was breast-feeding. (And here I've always been proud of being able to nurse and read at the same time!)

As soon as one Bad Mother fades from view, another quickly takes her place in the dock of the court of public opinion. Not long ago, the dingbat pop starlet Britney Spears was hoisted up as the latest agent of villainy. Her Bad Mother rap sheet is long and varied. It includes being committed to a psychiatric facility, losing visitation rights after failing to submit to court-mandated drug testing, driving with her infant son on her lap, and running in her car over the feet of photographers and sheriff's deputies. And apart from her legal troubles, there are her miscellaneous crimes of lifestyle. Her constant partying, her spendthrift ways ($737,000 every month!), and, most notoriously perhaps, her inexplicable refusal to wear undergarments. We can all agree, can't we, that Britney Spears is at best an incompetent mother and at worst a neglectful one. She's far worse than my first collar, the Medea of Muni, who pulled her daughter's hair on the J Church line. So why, then, do I find myself feeling like she's gotten a bit of a rough deal?

Perhaps because in a smaller way, at the periphery of the public eye, I was myself made to do the Bad Mother perp walk. For a Warholian fifteen I became fodder for the morning talk shows and gossip blogs, held up to scorn and ridicule as an example of maternal perfidy. My crime? Confessing in the pages of the *New York Times* style section to loving my husband more than my children.

In that essay I wondered about why so many of the women I knew were not having sex with their husbands, while I still was, and I concluded that it might be because they, unlike me, had refocused their passion from their husbands or partners onto their children. I wrote, "Libido, as she once knew it, is gone, and in its place is all-consuming maternal desire." And then I spent some time worrying about what was wrong with me: Why hadn't I successfully "made the erotic transition a good mother is supposed to make"? I said that if a Good Mother was one who loved her children more than anyone in the world, more even than her husband, then I was a Bad Mother, because I loved my husband more than my children.

The Bad Mother police were swiftly on the scene. They speculated publicly, down in the toxic mud of the comment sections on blog pages, that I was crazy, evil, a menace, that my children should be taken away from me. They cross-examined me on the set of *Oprah*. And New York City's elite Bad Mother SWAT team, the warrior shrews of UrbanBaby.com, sank their pointy little incisors into my metaphorical ankles.

I feel enough of Spears's pain to find myself wondering at the genesis of our current obsession with these varied archetypical manifestations of maternal evil. To a certain extent, of course, we've always been both terrified and titillated by the Bad Mother. Think Euripides' Medea and Agave, think Jocasta, think Joan Crawford. But I can't help but feel—and perhaps only because I've been tried and convicted of the crime—that there is something especially sharpened and hysterical about contemporary Bad Mother vitriol. The frequency with which a new Bad Mother is unmasked, and the extent of our interest in each one, are, I believe, more than merely symptoms of the contemporary general degeneration of civility. While, granted, the human dum-dum bullets of message boards like UrbanBaby hardly exemplify the attitudes of the civil and decent core of American society, they do seem to distill to a vile essence what is a widespread societal preoccupation with Bad Mothers.

There is an appealing sociopolitical rationale for our preoccupation with Bad Mothers, one articulated to me by the feminist scholar and advocate Lynn Paltrow, founder and executive director of National Advocates for Pregnant Women. Getting us to focus on Bad Mothers, she says, is part of a larger political agenda to keep our attention off the truth—that it is not our mothers but our government that has failed us. The patriarchy and its political, media, and profit-making machines encourage us to scapegoat and vilify one bogeymama after another, because worrying about egregious freak-show moms like Wendy Cook and Britney Spears distracts us from the fact that, for example, President George W. Bush cheerfully vetoed a law that would have provided health insurance to four million uninsured children.

As persuasive as I find Paltrow's argument, something in me rebels at the notion that we can attribute our communal obsession primarily to the patriarchy. I agree with her that we are just at the very beginning of accepting the notion of gender equality (it's only been, as she says, "a microsecond in the course of history"). Still, the blare of condemnation that drowns out so much of civil discourse on the subject of mothering and child rearing originates not from some patriarchal grand inquisitor's office but, in large part, from individual women. And while women have always, historically, been the enforcers of acceptable social conduct, even when it was to their detriment (remember Abigail Williams, the lead accuser in the Salem witch trials?), an hour or two surfing the myriad of mommy blogs provides compelling support for the notion that, in this area at least, we women are the primary authors of our own subjugation. The Bad Mother cops with the most aggressive arrest records are women.

And why? Because the Andrea Yateses and Susan Smiths, the "crack hos" and the welfare moms, provide us with a profound personal service. By defining for us the kinds of mothers we're not, they make it easier for us to stomach what we are.

When I polled an unscientific sampling of my friends and family, they had no trouble defining what it meant to be a Good Father. A Good Father is characterized quite simply by his presence. He shows up. In the delivery room, at dinnertime (when he can), to school recitals and ball games (whenever it's reasonably possible). He's a good provider who is not above changing a diaper or wearing a Baby Björn. He's a strong shoulder to cry on and, at the same time, a constant example of how to roll with the punches. This definition seems to accommodate, without contradiction, both an older, sentimentalized *Father Knows Best* version of a dad and our post–*Free to Be You and Me* assumptions.

However, my polling sample had a difficult time describing a Good Mother without resorting to hyperbole, beneath which it's possible to discern a hint of angry self-flagellation.

"Mary Poppins, but biologically related to you and she doesn't leave at the end of the movie."

"She lives only in the present and entirely for her kids."

"She has infinite patience."

"She remembers to serve fruit at breakfast, is always cheerful and never yells, manages not to project her own neuroses and inadequacies onto her children, is an active and beloved community volunteer; she remembers to make playdates, her children's clothes fit, and she does art projects with them and enjoys all their games. And she is never too tired for sex."

"She's everything that I'm not."

These responses might be colored by the fact that my polling sample, despite containing a moderate amount of racial, religious, and socioeconomic diversity, was composed of women of approximately the same age (mid-thirties to early forties) and the same level of education (which can be described, succinctly, as "more than they use"). Nonetheless, the common elements in the responses make a compelling statement both about the pervasive power of the antiquated June Cleaver vision of motherhood and about how badly we fall short.

The single defining characteristic of iconic Good Motherhood is self-abnegation. Her children's needs come first; their health and happiness are her primary concern. They occupy all her thoughts, her day is constructed around them, and anything and everything she does is for their sakes. Her own needs, ambitions, and desires are relevant only in relation to theirs. If a Good Mother takes care of herself, it is only to the extent that she doesn't hurt her children. As one of my polling samples put it, "She is able to figure out how to carve out time for herself without detriment to her children's feelings of self-worth." If a Good Mother works, she does so only if it doesn't harm her children, or if her failing to earn an income would make them worse off. More important, even the act of considering her own needs and desires is engaged in primarily to make her children into better people. As one woman told me, "A Good Mother is in shape and works outside of the home so she can be a good role model."

Being a Good Father is a reasonable, attainable goal; you need only be present and supportive. Being a Good Mother, as defined by mothers themselves, is impossible. When asked for an example of a Good Mother, the women I polled came up with June Cleaver and Marmee, from *Little Women*. Both of whom are by necessity, not coincidence, fictional characters. The Good Mother does not exist, and she has never existed, not even in those halcyon bygone days to which the arbiters of maternal conduct never tire of harking back. If the producers of *Leave It to Beaver* had really wanted to give us an accurate depiction of late-1950s and early-1960s motherhood, June would have had a lipstick-stained cigarette clamped between her teeth, a gin and tonic in her hand, and a copy of *Peyton Place* on her nightstand. But still, this creature of fantasy is whom the mothers in my sample measured themselves against, and their failure to live up to her made them feel like Bad Mothers.

It's as if the swimmer Tracy Caulkins, winner of three Olympic gold medals, setter of five world records, were to beat herself up for being slower than the Little Mermaid.

Without exception, the mothers I know feel like they have failed to measure up. As Judith Warner so eloquently wrote in her book *Perfect Madness: Motherhood in the Age of Anxiety*, "This widespread, choking cocktail of guilt and anxiety and resentment and regret . . . is poisoning motherhood."

I have been pondering the reasons for this maternal anxiety ever since I first found myself suffering from it, sitting in a playground, my briefcase traded in for a diaper bag, my focus narrowed to my baby and myself, my ambition curdling into something I thought was anger but I now realize was closer to despair. I had always been hard-driving and ambitious, myopically fixated on my career. But I was working long hours, and after a day taking care of desperately needy people who looked to me to keep them from spending years, decades, or even the rest of their lives in jail, I had nothing left for my baby. I was jealous of Michael, a work-at-home writer who got to spend long, languid hours with our daughter, dressing her up in her new outfits and shuttling her from Mommy & Me to the library. One day I simply packed up my desk, tossed my framed diplomas into the attic, and became a stay-at-home mom.

It was everything that I thought it would be. Mommy & Me, story time at the library, Gymboree, long stroller walks with my stay-at-home-mommy friends. And then the next day it was Mommy & Me, story time at the library, Gymboree, and long stroller walks with my stay-at-home-mommy friends. And the day after that, and the day after that, and the day after that.

Within a week I had gone mad.

I took a certain satisfaction in the fact that I was now the most important person in the day-to-day life of my child, but I was also bored and miserable. And the fact that I was bored and miserable terrified me. A Good Mother is never bored, is she? She is never miserable. A Good Mother doesn't resent looking up from her novel to examine a child's drawing. She doesn't stare at the clock in music class, willing it along with all the power of a fourth grader waiting for recess. She doesn't hide the finger paints because she can't stand the mess. A Good Mother not only puts her children's needs and interests above her own but enjoys doing it. If I wasn't enjoying myself, then I wasn't a Good Mother. On the contrary, I was a bad one.

The intense Bad Mother anxiety felt by me and by so many of the women I know has everything to do with what the journalist Peggy Orenstein, author of *Flux: Women on Sex, Work, Love, Kids, and Life in a Half-Changed World*, calls "making pre–Betty Friedan choices in a post–Betty Friedan universe." When we were little girls—we daughters of the late 1960s and the 1970s—none of us said we wanted to be wives and mothers when we grew up. None of us said we wanted to run the nursery school committee or frost perfect cupcakes or spend our days ferrying children back and forth from hockey games to music classes. We all had ambitions that went beyond the confines of our own houses. We wanted to work, to have careers, to have professions. But for so many of us, the realities of the workplace and of family life have either defeated or drastically changed these expectations. When career advancement demands a sixty- or seventy-hour workweek, when the child-care bill approaches or exceeds your paycheck, or when simple survival requires a second job, juggling home and family suddenly shifts from the challenging to the impossible. Someone usually ends up sacrificing his or her career to some extent, and in a world where a woman still earns roughly seventy cents to a man's dollar, and where a man's identity is still almost exclusively defined by what he does, that someone is almost always the mother.

So here we are, either staying home or making serious professional compromises in order to be more available to our children or feeling like terrible mothers for having failed to make those sacrifices. I imagine there are some mothers who have without regret channeled all of their ambition and energy into making homemade Play-Doh, organizing the nursery school capital campaign, and directing the fifth-grade social committee, but I have never met one. Most of the women I know feel an underlying and corrosive sense of disappointment and anxiety. The women I know are, on some level, unfulfilled. And the women I know spend a lot of time trying to avoid wondering whether the sacrifice was worth it.

13

It's that very wondering, it's the being unfulfilled, that makes us feel the worst. That's what triggers our most intense anxiety. Feeling dissatisfied, bored, and unhappy is unpleasant, yes, but what really scares us is the very *fact* of our dissatisfaction, boredom, and unhappiness. Because a mother who isn't satisfied with being a mother, a mother who wants to do more than spend her days with her children, a mother who can imagine more, is selfish. And just as the Good Mother is defined by her self-abnegation, the single most important, defining characteristic of the Bad Mother is her selfishness.

Even if we sympathize with Andrea Yates's postpartum depression, even if we've suffered from it ourselves, even if we are ready to acknowledge that homeschooling five children in a converted school bus would probably on its own be enough to drive us to homicide, we condemn Yates for having succumbed to her despair. She valued her own misery more than her children's lives. We condemn the Bad Mother even when she is the primary victim of her own tragedy, like, for example, Carol Anne Gotbaum, the Upper West Side mother of three who, while on her way to an alcohol rehabilitation facility, died in police custody after an altercation in the Phoenix airport. "Yes, I'm sure she was mother of the year," snapped an UrbanBaby mom-squad assassin, after someone wrote a sympathetic post about Gotbaum, "what with her severe alcoholism, suicide attempts, and tendency towards verbal abuse." Another deemed the entire incident an example of "self-indulgent nonsense."

When Susan Smith drove her two children into a lake, one of the most compelling facts about the case, one reported in the press over and over again, was that she had allegedly done so because the man she was dating didn't like kids. Here was this woman who was clearly insane, but the media narrative about her was that she valued the satisfaction she got from her lover, she valued his wealth and attention, more than she valued her children's lives. Instead of getting a real analysis of the psychology of her crime, we were told that Susan Smith killed her children in order to be loved, and to be rich. Selfish bitch.

Even the maternal crimes of idiot starlets like Britney Spears amount essentially to selfishness. She'd rather go out to clubs than take care of her kids. She'd rather sleep in than report for her drug tests. She's spoiled rotten, and a rotten mother because she's so spoiled.

Not long ago I reread *Anna Karenina*, in Richard Pevear and Larissa Volokhonsky's magnificent new translation. In the novel there is an achingly sad scene where Anna, who has abandoned her husband and beloved son to be with her lover, excoriates herself with the worst insult she can imagine—she's an unnatural mother. A natural mother, one who understood the relative insignificance of her own happiness, would never have indulged it. Most of us are, obviously, not about to fling ourselves beneath the wheels of a locomotive, but the fear of being an unnatural mother, a Bad Mother, is all too familiar to us. We are supposed not only to sacrifice ourselves for our children but to do so willingly, cheerfully, and without ever feeling any seething resentment, and when we fail, as we must, we feel guilty and ashamed.

The question becomes: How does one find consolation in the face of all this failure and guilt? One way is by reveling in the dark exploits of mothers who are worse, far worse, than we are. We obsess about these famous bogeymamas; we judge ourselves for a little while not against the impossible standard of the Good Mother but against the heinous Bad Mother. The more rigid the prescription of the Good Mother is, and the more complete our failure in emulating her, the more extreme the Bad Mother needs to be. Terrified of our own selfishness and failures, we look for models further on the spectrum from ourselves than we are from the Good Mother. We may be discontented and irritable, we may snap after the sixty-seventh knock-knock joke, our kids may watch three hours of television a day because we're too afraid, after checking our local map of sexual offenders, to send them outside to play, we may have just celebrated the second anniversary of the last time we had sex with our husbands, we may have forgotten to bring a snack to the playground, or, God forbid, brought a snack replete with partially hydrogenated vegetable oils, we may be divorced from our children's fathers, our children may not have fathers, our kids may sleep in our beds, our kids may not sleep in our beds, we may bottle-feed, or we may breast-feed for too long, our kids may score in the twelfth percentile on the verbal-reasoning section of the Iowa Tests, we may feed our kids peanut butter or strawberries too early and give them allergies, we may be so vigilant about not feeding them anything allergenic that they refuse to eat anything that's not white, we may yank on our daughters' ponytails while we are combing their hair, we may feel like the world notices and keeps track of each and every one of our maternal failures, but at least we're not Andrea Yates or Susan Smith. We're not Wendy Cook or Britney Spears. Hell, we're not even Ayelet Waldman.

That is, *you're* not.

Another strategy some of us have come up with to deal with our sense of failure and guilt is to rebel, to embrace the very identity we are afraid of, to loudly proclaim ourselves bad moms. We bad moms proudly wear our ambivalence on our sleeves. We vociferously resist and resent the glorification of the self-abnegating mother. We snarl at the mention of Dora the Explorer or Raffi. We shrug at the orange Cheetos dust smeared across our children's mouths. We swap stories of our big-box travails ("Your kid ran away from you at Target? That's nothing. I yelled at mine in the parking lot of Ikea and someone called the cops!"). We commiserate about how much we loathe the wannabe Good Mothers with their aggressive school volunteering, their Bugaboo strollers, and their Petunia Pickle Bottom diaper bags. We even confess that on rare occasions, and only under duress, we spank our children.

We bad moms are happy to confess our sins because we're confident that those who come closest, and with the most sanctimony, to emulating the self-effacing, self-sacrificing, soft-spoken, cheerful, infinitely patient Good Mother are the *real* Bad Mothers. After all, what is a child like whose mother has sacrificed herself on the altar of his paramount importance? What is a child like whose mother has selflessly devoted herself to his every need and desire? Is he thoughtful and kind, empathetic and liable to put others' needs before his own? Or is he so packed full of self-esteem, so conscious of his own sense of entitlement, that he is impossible to be around? Our children may wear unmatched socks, we trumpet, but they're better people than yours are.

The vogue for honesty, for exposing and embracing the ugly side of motherhood, is not a new thing. As far back as Erma Bombeck's weekly columns or Peg Bracken's *I Hate to Cook Book*, women have been attempting to derive comfort from the act of ruefully confessing their maternal failures. One seminal text of the bad-mom movement, for example, Anne Lamott's *Operating Instructions*, published in 1993, describes a mother who clings to sleep so fiercely that she doesn't even notice when her baby falls into the crack between her bed and the wall. Salon's Mothers Who Think page debuted in 1997 as a forum for this kind of resistance, although it sometimes functioned as its opposite. The literary an-

thology *The Bitch in the House* is a Bad Mother's manifesto, as are
the stacks of volumes with cutely sour titles like *Confessions of a
Slacker Mom* and *Mommies Who Drink*. I began my career as a
writer by publishing a series of murder mysteries—the Mommy-
Track mysteries—about a mother so bored with staying home with
her small children that she turns to solving crime just to keep herself from losing her mind. As an antidote to the Web sites
UrbanBaby and Babble, the Bad Mother movement offers up the
delightfully bilious Crabmommy and Heather Armstrong's Dooce,
who writes that "most days with a toddler are the emotional equiv-
alent of running over your skull with a car."

We bad moms defy the world to come up with an accusation
we have not already leveled against ourselves. Beating our critics
to the punch is certainly effective as a way of short-circuiting attacks. How much do they think it hurts me to be accused of being
a Bad Mother when that is the name of my book? But in our conscious rebellion, we bitches and slacker moms are as focused on
the Bad Mother archetype as any of the vigilantes of the Bad
Mother goon squad. If we truly didn't care, we wouldn't be writing
all these articles, memoirs, and books. We wouldn't be blogging.
We don't insist that we're Good Mothers despite our failings. On
the contrary, we seem to be saying only, okay, yeah, we're bad. So
what?

Despite the effectiveness of this technique, despite its power to
inoculate you against attack, it allows you to define yourself only
in negative terms. We don't call the entire project of identifying
Bad Mothers into question; we simply embrace the role. And in
the end, there is something hollow in that. There is no inherent
nutritional value in the antidote to poison.

Moreover, if examined too closely, all this defiance starts to ring false. I may be defiant about my failures and my selfishness, but I still feel guilty. I still feel bad. As happy as I am to crown myself Queen of the Maternal Damned, part of me still believes that my children would be better off with June Cleaver.

Is there really no other way to be a mother in contemporary American society than to be locked into the cultural zero-sum game of "I'm Okay, You Suck"?

Despite the Internet, the enabling technology that makes it ever easier for us both to judge others and to internalize our own self-judgment, couldn't we at least attempt to forge a positive and humane attitude toward mothers, one that takes into account their welfare as well as that of their children? Or is that an impossibly naive idea, the very consideration of which dooms me to be bitch-slapped by the meta-hypocrites of Gawker under the headline "Ayelet Whines: Can't We All Just Get Along?"

It shouldn't be that hard. We possess, after all, a perfectly adequate model, one that operates smoothly, almost imperceptibly, without engendering vitriol or causing much pain: the Good Father. There are no "daddy wars," and while Alec Baldwin and Michael Jackson have both served their time in the Bad Father stocks, it is rare for a father to feel that his own identity is implicated in or validated by their offenses. Self-flagellation is not the crux of the paternal experience.

I'm not calling for a national lowering of maternal standards to the rather minimal level considered acceptable by society for fathers. In fact, if more were expected of fathers, mothers might not end up shouldering such an undue burden of perfection. But it's hard enough to minister to the needs of children without trying to live up to an impossible standard at the same time. It's hard enough to achieve a decent balance between work and home without feeling like our inevitable mistakes are causing our children permanent damage. It's hard enough to braid a kid's hair on a moving train without worrying about an audience of censorious commuters.

Can't we just *try* to give ourselves and each other a break?

2. The Life She Wanted for Me

Before I had children, I knew exactly what kind of mother I would be: my mother had told me. She was a feminist of the 1970s consciousness-raising, pro-choice-marching, self-speculum-wielding school, and she expected me to fulfill her own ambitions, which had been thwarted by a society that resisted viewing a woman in any sphere other than the domestic, and by an imprudent marriage. My mission as her daughter was to realize the dream of complete equality that she and her fellow bra burners had worked so hard to attain.

My mother met my father the summer before she entered graduate school. Fifteen years older than she, he had custody of four children from his first marriage. His oldest child, a son, was only ten years younger than my mother.

When my mother went off to graduate school, my grandparents breathed a sigh of relief. Then, in a moment of utterly uncharacteristic romantic grandeur, my father sent my mother a telegram that said, "I'm pregnant. Come marry me." To me, the text of this telegram has always smacked of a calculated attempt to mask, with charm and humor, his very practical need. From the vantage point of decades, it seems clear that the subtext of the telegram was, "My children are running wild, driving me crazy, and I need a wife to take care of them!"

My parents have been married forty-four years, and my mother has never once described the story of their engagement, telegram and all, as anything other than the beginning of a mistake. When I ask her why she threw everything aside to marry a man so much older, with four difficult children and no steady source of income, sometimes she says it was because she was swept away by love—he was handsome, charming, a war hero. Sometimes she says that she was afraid, at twenty-two, of becoming an old maid, or that her best friend had just married an older man with four kids, and that made it seem like a less crazy thing to do. She always says that she realized almost immediately that she had made a mistake, but by then she was already pregnant with me—fecundity runs in my family—and it was too late. And even if she had the madness or the courage to take her baby and make her escape, there were those four motherless children to consider. She couldn't abandon them.

Not long after I was born, my mother discovered Betty Friedan. Had *The Feminine Mystique* been published a few years earlier, my mother's life might have been very different. She might have had a fulfilling career, instead of working at a series of frustrating and uninspiring jobs. She might never have married my father; she might have stayed at the University of Michigan, become a professor of art history or a museum curator. She might not have backed into a career as a hospital administrator because she happened to be working in a health clinic when someone finally realized that she was too smart to be relegated to typing and filing.

My mother struggled for her entire life to find professional satisfaction. She worked for men who were neither as intelligent nor as qualified as she was. She watched the steady rise of women just a few years younger, women who refused to settle, who refused to subsume their ambitions to a sexist world. She was angry—and is angry still—about the mistakes she made, and she was determined that I would not make similar ones. She raised me to believe not only that I was capable of anything but that I had an obligation—to myself, to society, most of all to her—to succeed. My future—a term I understood to be synonymous in her mind with "career"—was meant to fulfill her ideology and redeem her own frustrated professional and personal life.

That I was to have children was a given—feminist or not, she's a Jewish mother after all—but my career was to be paramount. Family would follow, and would be integrated, seamlessly and without challenge, into my life. She wasted no time in wondering whether I would be a Good Mother—that was a given—what was important was that I would be a *working* mother. Or, rather, a successful professional who just happened to have children.

At heart, and despite my occasional behavior and my frequent protestations to the contrary, I was a nice Jewish girl, and I wanted to please my mother. Moreover, I believed in her causes as fervently as she did. I accompanied her to pro-choice demonstrations, I helped her leaflet the neighborhood on behalf of liberal Democratic candidates for office, I responded with appropriate horror when kids showed up at school wearing "Students for Reagan" T-shirts. Most important, I did well enough in school to get into a good college, and although I betrayed her by refusing to attend her beloved Swarthmore, Wesleyan University was still an adequate sticker for the rear window of her car. A few years later, her red Aspen station wagon became unto a chariot of the gods when she was able to decorate its window not just with Wesleyan and Swarthmore stickers but with that most powerful of Jewish-mother incantations: Harvard Law School.

In college, I discovered my own brand of feminism, one that for a time involved great quantities of body hair and an intense program of sexual experimentation. My cousin Marcie had the misfortune of getting married during this period of my life, an event I celebrated in a strapless pink taffeta gown accessorized with two tufts of wiry black armpit hair.

My mother was so proud of me during those years and the ones that followed. I will never forget the expression of pure joy on her face when, in my very first year out of law school, my salary was higher than my father's.

My mother taught me that ambition was my right and my duty, and that I needed to be careful to structure my life in order to accommodate it. One of the keys to creating the life she wanted for me was to find a mate who would be a willing foot soldier in my battle for equality. I needed a husband who would value my professional identity as much as his own, who would assume half the household and child-care duties. Who would, if anything, subsume his ambitions to mine. I needed, in short, a man different from my father.

My father doesn't think of himself as sexist, and neither, really, do I. Born in 1925, he is no more nor less than a man of his time. It never occurred to him that his wife's career should have or could have been taken as seriously as his own. If asked, he would probably say that it was merely a function of earning capacity. He made more money than my mother, thus his job was more important. As strapped as they always were, it would have been foolishness to behave otherwise. If he was offered a better position two hundred miles away, then they had to move, whether or not she was working at the one job she ever really loved.

Like most men his age, my father is inept at managing the most basic details of their domestic life. He doesn't clean—I'm pretty sure he lumps toilet brushes and mops into the same "feminine products" category as tampons and vaginal deodorant—and he cannot cook. The only time I remember him preparing supper was during a week my mother spent in the hospital after surgery, and he served us salami and eggs every single night. Sometimes when he was feeling particularly cheerful, he would pack our school lunches for us, but as neither my younger brother nor I could gag down his peanut butter and butter sandwiches, we learned soon enough how to fend for ourselves. Left to his own devices, my father would subsist on a diet of Fudge Stripe cookies and orange juice mixed with Coca-Cola, in a room stuffed with teetering piles of ancient newspapers and dusty old books. The telephone would be buried in the cracks of the sprung sofa, next to the long-lost remote, but he would have noticed the absence of neither, because he would no longer be wearing his hearing aids.

"Do not marry a man like your father," my mother instructed. And, having been a witness to her frustration and their discord, and though I love my father dearly, I was eager to comply.

Men unlike my father abounded at Wesleyan University. They sat next to me in women's studies classes, playing with their long, stringy ponytails and wiggling the toes that peeped from beneath the straps of their Birkenstocks. They linked hands with me at silent vigils in front of fraternity houses that had committed the thought crime of showing porn movies during pledge week. They toted around the collected poems of Marge Piercy and well-thumbed copies of Gyn/ecology by Mary Daly. They wore T-shirts that proclaimed their opposition to apartheid and their membership in PETA, and they spoke with authority about Hélène Cixous and the feminist post-structuralist critique of phallogocentrism. These were precisely the kinds of men my mother had instructed me to marry (although whether they actually planned to practice the domestic equality they proposed was anyone's guess).

Unfortunately, over and over I failed to muster up any attraction for those earnest men in their huaraches and drawstring pants. I tried to sleep with them, to survive their passive, tentative, and overly deferential lovemaking. But they were so *boring*.

So I took a page out of the book of bossy women everywhere. I found myself a weak-willed man to push around, a man like the husband in my favorite Jewish joke. A boy comes home from school one day and says to his mother, "Mama, Mama, I got a part in the play!" "I'm so proud of you, darling," she says. "What part did you get?" The son puffs up his chest and says, proudly, "I'm the Jewish husband!" "The Jewish husband?" the mother says, aghast. "You just march back to school and demand that they give you a *speaking* role!"

Cast in the role of silent husband was my first serious boyfriend, a kindhearted and weak-willed Israeli I'll call Elan.* Elan deferred to me in all things. When we first started dating, I promised to move to Israel, but when I grew disenchanted with this idea, he obligingly followed me to Cambridge. While I was in law school, he got a job in a moving company, the default occupation of those Israeli immigrants who are not interested in the electronics business. We both knew that he'd never earn much of an income, so our plan—my plan—was that I would support us as an attorney, and he would take care of the children. It was the kind of plan my mother would approve of. (Or so you would have thought. It turned out, however, that a kibbutznik with no apparent aspirations beyond his high-school diploma was not what she wanted for me. Jewish motherhood, it turns out, trumps feminism.)

---

*My family, accustomed as they are to being fodder for my writing, has agreed to let me use their real names, but I've changed everyone else's, mostly because I'm hoping they won't recognize themselves. This is, by the way, not an unrealistic expectation. People almost never do. And then there are the others who come up and say, with a knowing laugh, "Wow, you really nailed me." Which may be true, except that I haven't the slightest idea who they are.

The plan was laid, the plan should have succeeded, but in the end the very thing that made it possible, Elan's tractability and lack of personal ambition, doomed it. It turned out that while the role of bossy wife came naturally to me, it didn't make me happy. *He* didn't make me happy, and I made him miserable, too. In law school, for the first time, I found myself surrounded by different kinds of men. If they wore huaraches, it was because they had spent the year of their Fulbright fellowship in Oaxaca organizing farmworkers. They'd trimmed their ponytails when they'd gone to work as legislative aides to Barney Frank and Tom Harkin. I met men like Barack Obama, one of my classmates, whose brilliant future seemed assured even then. Harvard Law School was replete with men who harbored the not-so-secret ambition to be president, each of whom had the confidence of a Heisman Trophy winner considering his future in the NFL.

That ambition, that confidence, turned out to be much more alluring than a placid willingness to defer to your wife. I broke up with Elan and turned my attentions to those ambitious men, and to my own career. And then, one day, after being dumped by a religious Catholic who doubted, quite wisely, that I would allow our children to be raised in the Church, my roommate's best friend suggested that I go on a blind date with a buddy of his from high school. I had just finished retelling, with great drama and a few tears, the tale of my rejection at the hands of the observant Catholic. Jon smiled sympathetically and said, "I know a Jewish guy who'll date you."

When Jon called Michael to tell him about me, Michael was suspicious of the whole enterprise.

"A blind date?" he said. "I don't think so."

Jon said only, "Your loss," and changed the subject. Michael says now that it was the very casualness of Jon's reply that sparked

27

his curiosity. Jon says what sparked Michael's curiosity was that Jon told him I had a nice rack.

(How well I remember that rack! Those perky breasts that hovered just below my chin. Those pert nipples. That swelling cleavage. After four children and a full seventy-two months of breast-feeding, the last six of which were spent with my nipples clamped in the death vise of a breast pump, it is only by dint of foundation garments designed by teams of MIT professors who otherwise spend their days drawing up plans for the world's longest suspension bridges that my breasts achieve a shape even approximating round. When I undue the clasps, buckles, straps, and hoists of these miraculous feats of engineering, my boobs tumble to the ground like boulders falling off a cliff. I could polish my shoes with my nipples.)

I consulted with my girlfriends about attire. Casual but sexy was the consensus. One friend lent me her perfect jeans, the ones that cinched tight at the waist and showed off her ass (this was 1992, long before we began wearing our jeans slung low on our hips). Another had the perfect black leather belt. I bought a new crisp white cotton blouse, polished my lucky black boots, and then was confronted with the most important sartorial dilemma of all. The rack about which Jon had raved had to be shown off to full advantage. That called for a new bra. White, lacy, and with enough push-up power to confirm his assessment.

The night of the date I tamed my unruly hair into submission, applied the right amount of makeup, and squirted myself with just a hint of scent. And I waited. And waited some more. And waited for a while after that. Forty-five minutes after our appointed time, when I was about to give up, tear my useless new underwear to shreds, and gobble up the contents of my freezer, my buzzer rang.

I was living at the time on Fourteenth Street and Avenue A,

an area of New York City that has since moved to hip, through fashionable, and on to staid. Back then, however, it was the kind of place where you crunched crack vials beneath your shoes every morning on the way to the subway, and were not infrequently awakened in the middle of the night by the sound of gunfire.

I tried to buzz Michael into the building, but the buzzer was, as usual, broken. Too impatient to wait for the elevator, I rushed down the stairs. There he was, standing in the entryway behind the glass door, his hair even wilder than in the photograph on the jacket of his books, his eyes even more blue, his smile goofy and broad. Bells didn't ring, angels didn't sing, but I did, indeed, fall in love at first sight. I know this because a single thought entered my head. "Now I can *finally* stop dating."

I am cynical and pessimistic, and I don't believe in love at first sight. I believe you have to know someone to love him, have to see his good and bad sides, his flaws and foibles. I believe that love grows, and that attraction or infatuation cannot be the basis of a real life together.

And yet.

There is a word in Yiddish—*bashert*—that translates more or less as soul mate. Intended. The one that God, or fate, meant for you. The legend associated with this word says that before you are born, an angel appears to the soul of your infant self and takes you on a tour of your life. You visit your future, or a version of your future. One of the things the angel shows you is the person whose soul is a match for yours. The person with whom you are meant to share your life. Then the angel strikes you beneath your nose, leaving that subtle channel in the skin between the nose and the mouth, your philtrum. The blow causes you to forget what you have seen. But there remains a vestige of memory, an unconscious sense of what you saw and learned. Enough of a memory to evoke a jolt of recognition when you stumble across your *bashert*. When, for example, you see him standing behind a pane of bulletproof glass, a bouquet of purple irises in his hand.

We went out to dinner, to a romantic restaurant with banquette seating and dim lighting. For the first and last time in our relationship, we drank an entire bottle of wine.*

After dinner and that unlikely bottle, we walked over to the Bowery. Somewhere between Spring and Prince streets Michael leaned over and kissed me. We kissed in that face-mashing, lip-groping way of teenagers. And we kept kissing. At Max Fish, an agonizingly trendy bar. At a tiny table in the Ukrainian café Veselka. On my corner. In my postage stamp of a lobby. In front of the elevator. We kissed and kissed and kissed. And then he left.

That's how I knew it was forever. It was the first time since I was approximately fifteen years old that I did not sleep with a man on our first date. That, and the fact that within the first hour of my meeting him, he told me that, because he was a writer and worked at night, he intended to spend his days taking care of his children, so that his wife could pursue her career.

Here he was, the man I'd been looking for all along, the man my mother had sent me out in the world to track down and bring home. Funny and smart, Jewish and successful. And harboring ambitions of being a househusband. He would take care of my chil-

---

*There are two kinds of Jews in the world, those who drink and those who don't. My grandfather was, by all accounts, the former. He liked his schnapps, he played the ponies, he bet on his beloved Brooklyn Dodgers. My parents, however, are the other kind of Jew. Their "liquor cabinet" was a single bottle of apricot brandy that resided on a high shelf in the kitchen, behind a wicker basket that once held a selection of Zabar's smoked meats and tins of nuts, and next to a coffeemaker with a broken carafe that still "worked perfectly well." That bottle of apricot brandy stood untouched, until one weekend during my senior year of high school when I drank the contents, drove to Great Adventure, and regurgitated every last drop across the chests of those adventurers unfortunate enough to experience with me the rules of inertia in the spinning rotor ride.

dren while I worked. He would be an equal parent and an equal partner. He would make it easy for me to be the kind of woman my mother and I had planned for me to be. Is it any wonder that I proposed to him three weeks after our first date?

Not only did he, dear reader, marry me, but he followed me first to San Francisco, where I had a clerkship with a judge, and then to Southern California, where I found my dream job, as a public defender, representing indigent defendants in federal court. His career was portable, mine was not, and, more important, my ambitions were every bit as important as his. To this day neither my mother nor I can believe our good luck.

I loved my job. I got off on every part of it—I was a natural defender, I reveled in my battles with opposing counsel, I enjoyed the intellectual challenge of arguing before the court, a jury trial was my idea of bliss. And, especially, I loved my drug-dealing, bank-robbing, gangbanging clients. The job was difficult, frustrating, and more fun than I'd ever had in my life.

I achieved the future my mother had struggled so mightily to ensure for me. A job I loved, and a man I loved. A man who did all the cooking and most of the housework. A man who was eager to start a family and planned to be the primary caretaker. My goals accomplished, my future assured, all I needed to do was sit back and reap the rewards.

The sense that I was doing exactly what I was supposed to be doing subsided not a whit when I became pregnant, although from the beginning the baby complicated things. I remember one day running lightly up the steps to the courthouse in my little blue suit and matching suede pumps and stopping suddenly. I gulped a few times and then leaned over the railing and threw up the entire contents of my stomach into the bushes before the bemused eyes of the jurors who were enjoying a quick cigarette before the trial day began. I debated asking the judge to instruct the jury that my queasiness resulted not from any lack of faith in my client but rather from my pregnancy. Instead, I contented myself with chewing ostentatiously on a stack of saltines throughout the trial. The judge, a mother herself, helped me by calling a recess whenever she caught me looking green around the gills.

Still, even though I was spending half my day kneeling in front of the toilet bowl and the other half adjusting my maternity pantyhose, it didn't occur to me that a baby would interrupt the scheme my mother and I had outlined for my life. On the contrary, I shamelessly made use of my pregnancy to curry favor with judges and juries alike. I encouraged my clients to pull out my chair or take my arm as I heaved my bulk around the courtroom. The jury reacted to this solicitude just as I wanted them to. They took one look at how sweetly the tattooed, methamphetamine-addled drug dealer took care of his adorable, little pregnant lawyer, and decided that he could not possibly be as bad as the prosecutor was making him out to be.

I worked until the very end of my pregnancy, until my feet were too bloated to fit into my pumps and my belly was so big that by the time I moved my car seat back far enough to accommodate my girth, I could no longer reach the brake pedal. When I finally went out on maternity leave, I didn't even bother cleaning up my office. I knew it would be only a matter of a few months before I returned.

During this period, on the rare occasions that I appeared in non-lactating public, I was invariably reminded of how important it was that I get back to work. Once, at a party, a successful female movie producer to whom I was introduced as "Michael Chabon's wife," as if that were the sum total of my identity, sized me up with a glance, taking in my swollen, leaking breasts, my quivering postpartum belly, the faded black maternity dress that was still the only thing in my closet that fit. With a pitying smile, she patted me on the arm and said, "I so envy you. I wish I'd been able to just give it all up and stay home with my daughter. Lucky you!"

Yes, lucky me, I thought. While you're busy making a series of monster box-office hits, including the most lucrative romantic comedy of all time, I'm spending my days analyzing the frequency and consistency of infant bowel movements. While you're totting up box-office receipts, I'm totting up ounces of pumped breast milk. And while you're evaluating the relative merits of different literary properties up for adaptation, I am—without irony—evaluating the relative merits of Huggies and Pampers. Lucky, lucky me.

I went back to work.

But not, as it turned out, for long.

I made myself a little sign for my office door. "Pumping, please knock." Three times a day I would put up the sign, and within three minutes the door would burst open and reveal one of the guys from the mail room bearing a stack of letters or an urgent fax. "Oh my God," he'd say. "Am I interrupting something?" It turns out that young men are unable to resist the temptation of bared breasts, no matter how pendulous and mapped with bright blue veins. The first few times I sprang back, grabbing for my blouse and spraying precious breast milk in all directions. But after a while I would simply roll my eyes and shove my nipples farther into the horns, as if the clear plastic provided any kind of conceal-ment. Why it never occurred to me to just not put up the sign, I have no idea. Perhaps because I refused to give up my belief in people's better natures, or perhaps because I was too addled by hormones to realize that the guys were matching their mail deliveries to my pumping schedule.

I made an art out of multitasking. I could do anything while pumping—research a motion, write a brief, negotiate a plea agreement. Figuring that a twenty-two-year-old slanger from the Raymond Avenue Crips 102 was not likely to recognize the rhythmic suck and hiss of a Medela Pump in Style, I even accepted collect calls from my clients in lockup while pumping. If they asked what was going on, I would fob them off with a puzzled "Noise? What noise? I don't hear anything."

The various frustrations and humiliations of pumping—the forty-five minutes spent with my nipples clamped in a vise in order to produce two ounces of watery blue milk, the embarrassment of being the object of the (truly) indiscriminate lust of postadolescent young men, the lugging of the pump back and forth, the incessant jocular comments ("Better label that clearly or someone will use it in their coffee, heh heh heh")—were not what led me to quit my job. What finally drove me out of the office and back to my baby was *jealousy*, bilious green envy. I was jealous of my husband, who spent his days with her, and I was jealous of my daughter, who spent her days with *him*.

There I'd be, crouched in my car trying to pump a few ounces before going into the Metropolitan Detention Center to explain to a client that he had less in common with O. J. Simpson and more with, say, Bruno Hauptmann, and Michael would call to tell me how cute Sophie looked playing in her new baby pool. I'd be stuffing Kleenex in my bra during court recesses, and Michael and Sophie would be enjoying a picnic lunch in the park. I'd be frantically finishing a sentencing memorandum, trying to convince the judge to overlook my client's really very short flirtation with that whole Aryan Brotherhood thing, and Michael would be reading Sophie *Goodnight Moon*, putting her down for her nap, and doing his e-mail.

I grew more and more frustrated with myself. I was confident that I was still doing a good job at work—I had a few important victories during this period, including the dismissal of a serious ten-year mandatory-minimum case against an innocent client (a rarity for a public defender—both the dismissal and the innocence). I was doing my job well. A competent, confident working mother, just as my own mother expected me to be. At least that's how it seemed.

Caring for my clients took a tremendous amount of emotional energy. So much so that even when I was able to get home at a reasonable hour, I found myself with little left to give to the person who was most entitled to my maternal devotion. I would walk in the door and dump my briefcase, my bag, and my pump just in time for Michael to pitch Sophie at my head like a football and take off for some downtime in his office. (In retrospect, perhaps I should have examined more closely the source of his early evening desperation.) After not seeing me all day, the baby wanted to play, she wanted to show me things, she wanted me to get down on the floor and roll around with her. This was not a baby who was interested in cuddling. She didn't want to snuggle up in her mother's arms. She wanted to *move*. But all I was capable of doing after my long day at work was lying there, virtually inert.

One night, in desperation, I turned on a videotape of *The Lion King*. To my surprise, Sophie scrambled up on the couch next to me, cuddled up, and sat, rapt and still, for the next eighty-seven minutes.

When I got home from work the next evening, she glanced at the television with a cocked eyebrow. Then she roared.

"Do you want to watch *The Lion King?*" I asked hopefully.

She roared again.

For the next month, every night after work Sophie would roar like a lion cub, I would pop in the video, and we would veg out in front of the television in a state of mutual, trancelike bliss. Until, finally, one day, the music came on and I began singing, and found that I was able, from memory, to recite the entire movie. All of it. Every song, every line of dialogue, from the first *"Nants ingonyama bagithi baba"* ("Here comes a lion, Father," for those of you who don't speak Swahili or are, perhaps, better parents than I) to the final "Circle of life, circle of life." I knew it all by heart. And Sophie, who otherwise possessed no more than the vocabulary one would expect of a precocious toddler, was right there with me.

I quit work the next day. My boss, one of the best lawyers I'd ever met, a woman with two children, a woman who had not allowed her babies to interfere with her career, a woman who had not betrayed her feminist mother, smiled at me and said, "Why don't you take a leave of absence?"

"No," I insisted. "I'm quitting. I want to stay home with my kid. I want to go to Gymboree and take her to the zoo. I want to put her down for her nap and be there when she wakes up. I want to be a full-time, stay-at-home mom."

"See you in a few weeks," she said.

I packed up my office, leaving nothing behind this time. I had no intention of returning.

I did not have the courage to break the news to my mother. Instead, I found a job teaching a class at Loyola Law School, a few hours once a week for about what I would have earned at Starbucks, and informed my mother that I was merely in the process of switching careers.

My mother was not pleased. She began a campaign to bring me

back to my senses, her initial concern swiftly turning into anger. What was I *doing*? Did I not understand that I was throwing it all away? I was going to regret it. I was going to be miserable. This would be the worst mistake I ever made. Did I not remember what had happened to her?

I dug in my heels. This was *my* decision, I told her. I had an obligation to my baby. I wanted to be there for Sophie (with the implication, of course, that she, my mother, who had gone back to work when I was a baby, had not been there for me). This was the right thing to do for my family, and nothing she said could dissuade me.

I never let her know that within a week of quitting my job at the federal public defender, I had already begun to lose my mind. There was no way I would admit to her that the sheer monotony of caring for a baby was killing me. It turns out that entertaining someone with a two-minute attention span for fourteen hours is infinitely harder than trying to convince a jury of Orange County Republicans that your illegal immigrant client had no idea that the cardboard box he was carrying contained eight kilos of cocaine. Negotiating with a prosecutor over a plea agreement had nothing on trying to convince a two-year-old to go down for a nap. And cross-examining a scumbag confidential informant was a whole lot easier than wrestling a howling child into her car seat when what she really wanted to do was have one more ride on the merry-go-round.

I wasn't prepared for how ill suited and poorly trained I was for the job of full-time mother. I was not accustomed to performing poorly. Whether because I'd so completely assimilated my parents' expectations or because I enjoyed both the fruit and the feeling of success, I had not, before I became a mother, had much truck with failure.

But almost as soon as I gave birth, I came to the sickening realization that this particular enterprise would be *defined*, for me, by failure. I failed every day. I forgot the baby wipes or the diapers at home. I forgot a change of clothes and ended up running into babyGap to buy a new onesie for my shit-covered baby. I didn't put on the Baby Einstein video, or I left it on for two hours more than the prescribed twenty minutes. I was short-tempered and unhappy, and I couldn't remember the Gymboree teacher's name.

Worst of all, I was bored. I was just absolutely and completely, soul-crushingly bored. The playground became this purgatory of swinging, swinging, swinging (whence this baby's infinite capacity for swinging? She was never willing to do anything else for more than eleven seconds), forgotten juice boxes, and upper lips encrusted with that ineradicable epoxy of sand and booger.

But it wasn't all bad. There were a myriad of moments so replete with joy that thinking back on them now makes me flush with pleasure. I remember with perfect clarity taking a bath with Sophie when she was about eighteen months old. I remember the rubbery plumpness of her skin, the slip of her body against mine. I remember the feel of her hands on my face as she fashioned me a bubble beard and matching hat. I remember the brilliant pink of her lips against the white of her own bubble beard. I remember the grip of her tiny toes as she dug them into my thigh. I remember the wriggling heft of her when the bath was over and I rolled her into a towel that covered her from head to toe.

I remember those moments, and I remember the day when I had, by some miracle, enough quarters in my pocket to allow her to ride the miniature merry-go-round in front of the grocery store. I remember rides one through six, and I remember the color of her face (beet red) when I told her that I had neither the time nor the quarters for a seventh. Her wail was piercing enough to frighten the pigeons, who abandoned their tussle over the bounty of the su-permarket Dumpster and took off into the air. It was piercing enough to attract the attention and the censure of the passersby. It was piercing enough so that when I wrenched her out of the sad-dle of the pink duck around whose fiberglass belly her legs were clamped so hard that they had to be pried free, it made my ears ring.

I hoisted her up on my shoulder, trying to avoid her wildly kicking legs and regretting my decision to buy those cute little sad-dle shoes with the hard soles instead of the less-likely-to-bruise Keds. Dragging my laden grocery cart behind me, I manhandled her over to the car. As I was shoving her into her car seat, she sud-denly stopped screaming. With a sneer the likes of which I wasn't to see for another decade, she warned, "Daddy's going to come home and see what's going on with Mommy and Sophie."

She was planning on snitching me out! And the worst part was that I knew I had no defense, other than that she was being a mis-erable brat and had pissed me off.

Another C– day. No maternal dean's list for me. Instead, I looked to be heading for detention. I should have listened to my mother.

But I have always been more stubborn than is good for me. Once I made the decision to stay home, once I decided that that was the right thing to do, I could not bring myself to concede defeat. I had made such a *point* out of it with my mother. I was doing the right thing, which by implication meant that she had not. I began to spend a lot of time ranting that we daughters of feminists had es-sentially been lied to. Our mothers and the professors of our women's studies courses had told us that it was our job to do it all, without warning us how impossible that task would be. What was needed, I said at the time, was a dose of realism.

I had spent my whole life up to that point working toward a goal set for me by my mother, a goal I had supported with unquestioning commitment. Suddenly not only was I questioning the goal, but I was no longer buying its very premise. I was still reacting to my mother's ambitions, but now, instead of living the life she'd intended for me, instead of redeeming her lack of options by embracing my own, I was turning my back on everything. I was turning into a housewife—albeit an incompetent one—the very misery she and her generation had rejected.

My mother could not, and still cannot, understand why I did what I did, why I left a job I loved and a career that I had worked so hard to attain. Still, my life and my choices have not proved after all to be such a disappointment to her. I gave that stay-at-home-mom thing my all, but only managed it for a couple of depressed years. Eventually I found something else to do, an ambition as consuming as the law, if not quite so demanding. I began writing when I was pregnant with Zeke, my second child, although I didn't publish my first novel until he was three years old.

I have organized my life so that, to a great extent, my children take priority over my work, but I do things like pack up and leave for two weeks on a book tour, or miss a school talent show because I'm on deadline. I still think my mother should have prepared me for how fundamentally impossible this juggling business is, but I'm glad she inspired me to keep looking until I found a man like my husband. I'm glad she made me expect equality. I'm glad she pushed me so hard, because had she not I would never have had the confidence to become a writer. My mother taught me chutzpah, a critical trait if you want to survive and succeed. It's true I wish she had not responded to my announcement of my fourth pregnancy with a horrified "Oh, Ayelet," but I love how proud she is of my work. She buys dozens of copies of every one of my novels and gives them to (forces them on?) all her friends, her co-workers, people she meets at the supermarket (or at the Obama for America office; my mother is still as political as she ever was).

I have two daughters now, whom I am no doubt burdening with my own set of expectations. Sophie and her little sister, Rosie, know that I expect them to have careers, that I expect them to marry men like their father, who will not foist upon them all the labor of raising the children and keeping the home. I boss them around like my mother bossed me.

I know that someday my daughters will chart their own courses, they'll make their own mistakes. They in their turn will have to figure out how to keep all those balls in the air, how to maneuver despite inevitable frustration and failure. But just as I burden my daughters with my expectations, I also try to remind them that jugglers invariably drop balls, and no matter the persistent criticism of the Bad Mother police, balls do bounce. When they fall, all you need to do is pick them up and throw them back up in the air.

3. Free to Be You and I

I spent a key portion of the 1970s stretched out on the shag rug of my parents' home in suburban New Jersey, clutching a pink record jacket in my hands, and singing lustily along with Marlo Thomas. *Free to Be You and Me* showed up in the house when I was about eight years old, and my mother immediately put it on constant rotation, supplanting Pete Seeger and Peter, Paul, and Mary on the family playlist.

With the exception of the grammatical (would it have killed them to call the record *Free to Fly, You and I?*) we took Marlo Thomas's lessons very seriously. My mother went out and bought my younger brother a doll, although he, unlike the eponymous hero of "William's Doll," *never* wanted one. Whenever I heard someone say the words "Ladies first," I chorused back, "And mighty tasty, too," making me seem like a lunatic, until I explained about the tender, sweet young thing and the tigers (which probably didn't, in retrospect, help much). My brother and I learned that it didn't matter if we were boys or girls; we didn't have to be pretty or grow tall. We didn't, in fact, have to change at all.

And we learned—from the three-pack-a-day rasp of Carol Channing—that when there was housework to do, we were to make sure that we didn't do it alone. Good mommies and daddies did their housework together.

About 250 miles away, on a shag rug in a living room in Columbia, Maryland, Michael was being taught the very same lessons. His mother's purchase of *Free to Be You and Me* coincided, perhaps not coincidentally, with her divorce. No longer able to rely on a comfortable future as a doctor's wife, my mother-in-law went back to school, first to finish college and then to earn a law degree, giving her significantly less time to manage the domestic details of the lives of her two sons. Michael was eleven when his father left, old enough to start helping around the house, regardless of his gender. Humming along to "Dudley Pippin and the Principal" and "It's Alright to Cry," he got busy cleaning up and cooking dinner. His chores at the time, in fact, significantly outnumbered my own, which consisted mostly of lackadaisically cleaning my room, walking the dog, and shifting a few dirty dishes from the table to the sink after dinner.

Michael's first marriage was to a woman who was similarly schooled in second-wave-feminist record albums, and thus, by the time we met, he was well trained to take on more than his share of the domestic duties. In the early days of our relationship, he used to say that he was the only husband in the world who had to pick up his *wife's* socks. I admit to having been a bit of a pig, something he teased out of me by the diminishingly amusing tactic of standing in front of the pile of my tossed-off clothes and saying, "Look! My girlfriend exploded." His mother taught him how to cook, thank God, because my own mother's lessons in that area went something like "Just dump the bottle of salad dressing on the cut-up chicken pieces and toss it in the oven."

To the delight of both of our mothers, we are in many ways living out Carol Channing and Marlo Thomas's dream. How important that has been to the success of our marriage I only really understood when I started to get responses to my notorious essay about loving Michael more than the kids.

Most of the feedback came in two varieties: (1) "Your kids

should be taken away from you, you cretinous bitch"; and (2) "Right on! That's how we've managed to stay married for fifty years." Every once in a while I receive e-mail from a pastor or priest congratulating me on following the injunction of Genesis 2:24 and cleaving unto my husband as a good wife should. And occasionally, I find winking in my in-box an e-mail from a man asking for advice on how to make his wife more like me.

I could and sometimes do reply with some version of "be careful what you wish for," but I know what it is that they are looking for. It's not that they want a crazy wife with a terrible temper who can neither cook nor change a lightbulb. They don't want a Weeble-shaped lover who not only wobbles but falls down. They certainly wouldn't enjoy having their personal lives splashed between the covers of books and magazines. What they want is to get laid.

The part of the essay that intrigues these men is where I wrote about how I am still interested in having sex with my husband. The men who write me these letters have wives like the women who sat in judgment of me on the set of *Oprah*. They have wives like the one who told the studio audience that she, unlike me, was a *Good* Mother, and on the very rare occasions when she let her husband "do his business," she watched television (*Jeopardy!*, not cable porn). I consider it a great personal victory that I managed to restrain myself from handing her a pair of pruning shears and saying, "Here you go, honey. Go ahead and snip it off at the base. You might as well finish the job."

The men write me, "Please tell me how to make my wife interested in sex again." Most of them reassure me (honestly or not) that they have not yet cheated on their wives, but the threat lies implicit in the e-mail. I just want some pussy, the more honest among them say. If she doesn't give it to me, can I really be blamed for looking for it somewhere else?

I know these men want me to give them some kind of magic spell, some words to incant or a particular gift to buy that will cause their wives to rip off their stretched-out sweatpants or high-waisted mommy jeans, toss their nursing bras into the trash, and slither into the scraps of lace and silk advertised on the cover of this month's Victoria's Secret catalog.

Save your money, I tell my male correspondents. If she's not sleeping with you now, you're not going to wake up her dormant libido by giving her a pair of tiger-printed crotchless panties. On the contrary. If you do, next Christmas you might find yourself the recipient of the gift of a twenty-class yoga card or a twelve-hundred-dollar Miele vacuum cleaner. It's a present, sure, but who's it really for?

What I tell these men is that if they are serious about wanting to salvage the erotic part of their marriages, they should unload the dishwasher. They should do a load of laundry (and fold it, too). There is nothing sexier to a woman with children than a man holding a Swiffer.

It can't come down to something as silly as that, can it? After all, as I wrote in the essay, it is not merely Michael's domestic prowess that inspires my devotion. I argued that I, unlike most women I know, have failed to make some kind of amorous transition, to supplant my husband with my children as the object of my passion. So yes, perhaps my advice to my correspondents is reductive, but the truth remains that one of the main reasons Michael is still so alluring after fifteen years of marriage, the reason I'd rather go to bed with him than do pretty much anything else in the world, is that I'm not angry. I'm not saying we don't fight. You bet we do. But I no longer suffer from that slow burn, that simmering fury that characterizes so many of the women I know, both stay-at-home moms and those with jobs that reward them with a salary.

Let me say (again) that I know that there are multitudes of women who are both sexually satisfied and deliriously happy with the choices they have made. There are also many (although I'll bet you not *multitudes*) whose husbands are equal partners in all aspects of their domestic lives. If you're one of those lucky people, you should just turn to the next chapter. This one's not for you.

This chapter is for those women—and the men to whom they are married—who have ended up, contrary to their expectations, living lives disturbingly similar to those of their mothers. Even the mothers who bought us the *Free to Be You and Me* albums never really expected that their husbands would take on half the child-care and household responsibilities. But we, their daughters, listened to the record and took for granted that our husbands would. This chapter is for the women who are surprised and, frankly, pissed off to find themselves, like their mothers before them, shouldering the bulk of the domestic burden.

It is kind of remarkable how little housework the men who marched next to me at the Take Back the Night vigils have ended up doing. Their approaches toward the work of caring for a family, while significantly more generous than those of their fathers, many of whom probably would have collapsed at the sight of a meconium-filled diaper, don't come close to parity.

Not long ago, the journalist Lisa Belkin published a cover story in the *New York Times Magazine* about how housework is shared by men and women in heterosexual relationships. She offered some numbers from a University of Wisconsin study: "The average wife does 31 hours of housework a week while the average husband does 14—a ratio of slightly more than two to one. If you break out couples in which wives stay home and husbands are the sole earners, the number of hours goes up for women, to 38 hours of housework a week, and down a bit for men, to 12, a ratio of more than three to one. That makes sense, because the couple have defined home as one partner's work. But then break out the couples in which both husband and wife have full-time paying jobs. There, the wife does 28 hours of housework and the husband, 16. Just shy of two to one, which makes no sense at all."

Frankly, I'm surprised by her surprise. That's certainly an accurate reflection of the relationships I know, and I live in *Berkeley*, a nuclear-free zone where the city council awards Code Pink a free parking space to make it easier for them to protest the Marine recruiting station. One would think that if any town had a significant proportion of adherents to "Equal Shared Parenting," it would be this one. And it's true that the cafés, the homeopathic pharmacies, the dog parks, and the aisles of Whole Foods are replete with men wearing drooling, gurgling fashion accessories strapped to their chests, men who are expert at slapping on a Seventh Generation chlorine-free diaper without tearing off the tabs, men who never miss a single back-to-school night (okay, maybe not that last one). It's just that most of those men don't spend their weekends cleaning the toilet (or arranging with the maid service to do it for them).

I just don't get it. I know Michael's and mine were not the only copies of *Free to Be You and Me* sold in the United States. Didn't those former little boys get the message? Or is it that menial household tasks are, for those of us who don't suffer from advanced cases of OCD, incredibly unpleasant? It was Carol Channing herself who told us, "Your mommy hates housework, your daddy hates housework, and when you grow up, you'll hate housework, too." Should it be a surprise that as soon as people are given the opportunity to opt out of it all, they do so? Is the problem not that men choose to do only a third of the domestic labor but that women let them? In other words, is this women's fault, too?

There is likely a grain of truth to that—I have often felt like shaking my most bedraggled and downtrodden friends and saying, "Stop *complaining*, just dump the kid on his lap and take a personal day." And plenty of husbands insist that when they try to do something around the house, they inevitably fail to accomplish the task to their wives' satisfaction.* So yes, women need both to ask for the help they need and to let go of their preconceptions about how a job should be done.† But perhaps if my correspondents want to get laid, demanding even more from their wives isn't the best way to accomplish that goal.

What men who describe spending an afternoon with their children as "babysitting" need to realize is that after an evening spent rushing from work to the grocery store, back home to cook dinner (or order it in—I'm a Jewish girl from the New York area, after all), then folding a load of laundry while supervising homework (and yes, thank you for doing the dishes, but it's not like you cured cancer; don't act like you deserve the Nobel Prize), before getting the kids to bed, packing their lunches for the next day, and then sitting down at the computer to answer twelve e-mails from the first-grade room parent about Pizza Day volunteers, fill out and submit the nursery school strategic plan survey, and create an Evite for the birthday party you've left yourself less than a week to plan, most women just aren't in the mood. And pretty much the same

---

*I'm as guilty of this as any wife. Never once has Michael loaded the dishwasher according to the system that it took me years—literally years—to perfect. More often than not, I shove him aside and redo it myself. Frankly, my method is quite clearly the only way to load a dishwasher, not to mention the only way to make sure the little arms don't snap off those French onion soup bowls. And it's not like I haven't given him detailed instructions about the system dozens, even hundreds of times. Honestly, how hard is it to remember to put the bowls on the top rack?

†With the exception, of course, of the aforementioned loading of the dishwasher. And folding towels, too. They just look better in the linen cupboard if you first fold them in thirds. And yes, even the washcloths, although I suppose I could muster a little flexibility on that issue.

goes for eighteen hours spent chasing and cleaning up after the kids, even without the workday crammed in there, too.

Most men I've talked to *understand* that the women in their lives are not interested in sex when they are feeling beleaguered and frustrated, but they don't really *get* it. The average man can be angry and frustrated with his wife, but still be perfectly happy to fuck her. The anger might even be just the pinch of Spanish fly he needs. Your typical man uses sex to unwind, while the last thing your typical woman wants when she's wound up is to have sex. Women—or most women, or some women, or the women I'm talking about, or maybe just women like *me*—do not find resentment erotic. On the contrary. If I am angry with you, or even just irritated, then the last thing I want to do is give you pleasure. I'll withhold it, even if that means I'm hurting myself, too.

Despite how it sounded to the men who read the article, it isn't like Michael and I haven't gone through our own periods of connubial drought. The postpartum hormonal swamp is nature's friendly way of trying to keep you from getting knocked up again, so that you'll be able to keep caring for the baby you already have. For the first couple of months after I gave birth, it was as if I were standing beneath a shower of estrogen, progesterone, and oxytocin, and not one of those environmentally correct low-flow showerheads, either. This was a spa deluge, dumping a hundred gallons a minute over my head. I would sooner have leaped into a shark tank full of starving great whites—while having my period—than have sex. Whatever sensual satisfaction I needed was amply provided by my sweet-smelling, plump, and delicious baby and the wash of oxytocin released every time he or she latched onto the breast. Even after the hormone flood had ebbed, breast-feeding was enough to keep me from wanting any other physical contact. I spent my days and nights at the baby's beck and call, my body and breasts available whenever the baby wanted them. The last thing I could tolerate in the few hours I had my body to myself was to give it to someone else. And don't even think of touching my breasts. If Michael accidentally brushed against my nipple while he was opening the car door for me, it took me a monumental exertion of will to keep from severing his hand at the wrist.

But even after these purely physical impediments to sex abated, there was a time when I still didn't want it. This was the period when I had left my job and was staying at home full-time. I was bored, and depressed, and had lost the sense of self that had kept me company over the last thirty years. I wasn't who I had once been, and I wasn't sure that I wanted to be who I was. Because I felt lost, I also felt ugly. Or at least unattractive. During this period I dressed disturbingly like my children, in overalls and T-shirts, stretchy pants and capacious blouses. It was as if I were advertising by my attire my sexual inaccessibility.

This was a particularly grim period in our marriage. Here we had made together these two babies, whom we both adored, who gave us such constant pleasure, for whom we shared such intense love that it sometimes felt like pain, and the two of us were further apart than we had ever been. I remember lying in bed next to Michael and telling myself that all I needed to do was take a page out of Queen Victoria's book and lie back and think of . . . well, not of England, nor of Berkeley, but of my marriage. But I couldn't bring myself to do it. I was too tired, it was too daunting, and although it took me a long time to realize this, I was too angry at him. I was too jealous.

Becoming a parent had not changed Michael's sense of himself, it had not destroyed his confidence, it had not made him feel lost. He definitely developed a new conception of his role in the world, but not one that was negative. That is not to say he didn't experience moments of panic. He marked the births of each of our children with a series of ailments. A few days before Sophie was born, he woke up in the middle of the night with chest pains. He felt like he had swallowed a ball. Convinced that he was having a heart attack, he had me rush him to the emergency room (I'll never forget the look on the guard's face when the hugely pregnant woman dropped her husband off at the entrance and then went off to park the car). An anxiety attack, diagnosed the doctor. As my pregnancy with Zeke progressed, Michael developed this floating blind spot in his left eye. Stress, the ophthalmologist said. No cure but to relax. With Rosie it was hives, with Abe it was hives *and* the blind spot. But even in the throes of these bizarre physical manifestations of his provider anxiety, Michael still knew who he was. If anything, he felt more sure of his place in the world. He had to continue doing what he was doing, because now he had a family to support.

I, on the other hand, was supposed to be doing this Good Mother thing, this caretaking thing, this Gymboree and Music Together and baby-massage thing, but unlike Michael, I wasn't happy filling my traditional domestic role. It didn't feel like I had come into some deeper understanding of what it meant to be a woman and a mother. It just felt like I'd gone astray, that I was stuck in a hole I had dug for myself, a hole I was not supposed to want to escape. And complicating all this was the fact that I *loved* these children so much. They were adorable and sweet and a never-ending source of sidesplitting amusement. I have never laughed as hard as I did the day, for example, that I caught Sophie dipping Michael's toothbrush into the toilet, with a seriousness of purpose that approached that of an EPA inspector testing Lake Michigan for PCPs. (Oddly, Michael did not find this quite as amusing as I did.) The fantastically adorable image of her chubby two-year-old face peeping out of her dinosaur Halloween costume is one that I will forever be able to rely on to make me feel happy. But even so, even with all these moments of joy, I was still glum and irritable, and about as horny as a . . . well . . . as a depressed mother of small children.

In retrospect, it's hard for me to believe Michael hung in there through all this. Why he had faith that I would figure it out, I'll never know. But he always did. When I first experimented with writing, he was immediately supportive, even though he had been through one marriage that collapsed at least in part under the weight of literary competition. He never reminded me that I had made a toast *at our wedding* in which I promised never to be a writer, both so that I could provide him with a steady income and health insurance and so that he need never fear that his success would make me jealous. Instead, he just told me how great he thought my writing was, and encouraged me to keep going. He was relieved that I had found what I needed—the beginnings of an identity separate from that of mother to my children. I was relieved both that the fog was lifting and that I was happy again. And we were both certainly relieved that my interest in sex had come out of its long hibernation.

In light of the seriousness of the sense of dissatisfaction I describe, in light of how profound a problem a young mother's loss of sense of self can be, I know that it seems unduly lighthearted to prescribe as a solution merely that the men who write me those sad e-mails try to pick up a little of the domestic slack. But what kept Michael and me together through the worst of my stumbling was the sense that we were on the same team. He never seemed to be saying, "Well, you chose to make this bed, why should I have to lie in it?" He had learned his *Free to Be You and Me* lessons too well to make what some might see as a pretty reasonable request—if this is the division of labor that we've chosen, if I am to earn the bulk of the money like my father did, then I am entitled to expect you, like my mother, to make my home and care for my children.

There may be plenty of women who are fine with things that way, plenty of women who don't object to carrying the extra domestic load, who think of that as a Good Mother's task, even if they work as hard and earn as much money as their husbands. But it's at least possible that Carol Channing was right, that everyone hates housework. Taking care of a house and family is work that never ends; like Sisyphus's wife, you and your basket of laundry never reach the top of the mountain. Feeling like it's all—or mostly—your responsibility is depressing. And even if you buy into the system, it still makes you happy to have help. You inevitably feel warm toward someone who is clearly thinking enough about you to relieve you of part of your burden. It's at least possible that my male correspondents might find that if, when they get home from work, instead of taking an hour to decompress, they put down their briefcases or toolboxes, roll up their sleeves, and scrub the stain out of the sink or puree some bananas to feed to the baby, their wives might suddenly be much more content. Hell, the men might even find themselves treated to that holy grail of male pleasure, and not just on their birthdays.

I suppose that it is disingenuous to discuss menial household labor without acknowledging that many of us are spared at least some of the most unpleasant of those duties: we subcontract them. There are, of course, millions of people who don't have the resources to off-load their toilet scrubbing, just as there are people who on principle refuse to participate in a system that compels the lower economic classes to deal, like untouchables, with the filth of the higher. But I grew up in a decidedly middle-class house (with periods of real financial instability), and my mother did everything she could to find the money to hire a cleaner every other week. I think she just decided that if she were to come home from a long day at work, make dinner, and then set about scrubbing the floors and de-scumming the shower, she'd end up killing herself, and taking us along with her. During the headiest era of my mother's feminist phase, she even figured out a way to spare herself the bulk of the cooking; she and the other members of her consciousness-raising group formed a supper cooperative. Each day a different one of them would cook for the group, separate the food into individual family-sized portions, and drop them off at the others' houses.

My mother had help, and so I grew up with a series of women or cleaning services coming to the house once every two weeks for a couple of hours. I rarely met them—they came when I was at school—and my only real experience of their presence was the hours I spent grumbling the night before cleaning-lady day when my mother forced me to clean my room in anticipation of their visits. "I don't pay them to pick up after you" was the refrain.

When I moved in with Michael, he suggested that we avoid any discord about who was going to do the really gross jobs by hiring a cleaning service. We have had various amounts of help since then—weekly cleaners, babysitters, nannies—and while I am grateful to them beyond measure, I am never anything but uncomfortable with the idea of being a lady with, essentially, a maid. A friend once told me about hearing a conversation between two nannies in which one of them said, "You should always make the beds. These women aren't used to having servants, and they *love* it when you make the beds." The comment caused me a stomach-churning moment of recognition. Our kids' nanny *did* make our beds, and every time I walked into my bedroom and saw the crisp sheets and smoothed pillows, I felt a wave of gratitude and pleasure. Because I feel so guilty about hiring someone with less money to clean my house, and because I feel a certain amount of shame at the idea of being able to afford a cleaner, my relationships with these women (and they are almost always women, and often, though not always, from third-world countries) tend to be fraught. I find it incredibly difficult, for example, to fire anyone, and have more than once found myself in the situation of hiring a maid to secretly clean up after my other maid, because I felt too bad for the first one to fire her, even though she wasn't able to manage the job.

So yes, I pay someone to scrub my toilets (although as the mother of two boys with poor aim, there are plenty of times when I'm down on my knees with a brush and a bottle of organic, non-toxic, unscented, all-natural toilet cleaner). Still, with four children and a huge hairy dog, I could have a staff of three arrive at my house at 6:00 a.m. and not depart before midnight, and there would still be plenty for Michael and me to do.

Belkin's article on housework included a reference to a survey on the division of labor by a pair of Berkeley (surprise, surprise!) academics, and Michael and I decided, just for the hell of it, to fill it out. The questionnaire is called "Who Does What?" and while our results more or less conformed to our expectations, it highlighted a few improvements that we've since tried to implement, albeit with limited success.

The survey divides up all the chores of maintaining a family and a household and asks you to score how much of it you do, how much your partner does, and how you *would like* the work to be divided. The tasks in the survey include, among many others: shopping for and preparing meals, cleaning the house, making calls to family and friends, caring for the family car or cars, providing the income, financial planning, initiating lovemaking, determining the frequency of lovemaking (different category!), and deciding how involved to be in religious or community activities. After you're done scoring all those categories, the survey asks you to evaluate both your and your partner's competence at a series of tasks, including, again among many others: reading to your child, choosing toys for your child, doing your child's laundry, disciplining your child, talking to your child's doctor, and making playdates. Then it asks you a bunch of questions about how you feel about how much you do, and how you think your partner feels.

No surprises in the last category of questions. I'm basically thrilled with how much Michael does, and he thinks I'm doing my share. He's proud of how much of the housework and child care he does, and I think I'm a crappy mother. Sigh. How much self-awareness would it take for me to stop internalizing the chorus of the Bad Mother choir?

In the first two categories, we agreed that, for example, I score a 9 on laundry, and he scores a 1, he wipes me out in the putting-to-bed category, and we let the mow-and-blow guy deal with the garden. There was a moment of discord around the bill-paying item, but Michael was finally forced to acknowledge that having not paid a bill in fifteen years, he cannot possibly be said to have earned a 2. Gross overestimations were accordingly erased and the appropriate figure inserted. He wished I would get down on the floor and play with the kids more, I wished he took more responsibility for making their doctors' appointments.

I heartily recommend that my male correspondents take the survey. It manages to reveal essential truths about your marriage and family without—at least in our case—making you angry. It makes you realize how much there is to do, how really endless the tasks are, and how hard it is to imagine, whatever your circumstances, doing it alone. Gentlemen, maybe after doing that load of whites and getting the resulting blow job, you can do the survey with your wives. I promise you'll both learn something.

As many of my other (generally female) correspondents take great pleasure in reminding me, there are lots of ways in which I am hardly the ideal mother and wife, lots of ways in which my family surely suffers because of my ineptitude and personality defects. And it's not because of *me* that we manage this housework thing so well. It's Michael, and the mother who trained him, who are the engineers of our happiness. It's also not just the two of us (and, yes, the cleaning service) who do the work. We've expanded this notion of shared household responsibilities to our children. Every one of them, even the little one, has a job. Sophie sets the table for dinner, and provides unlimited babysitting services. Zeke takes the garbage to the curb every week, clears the table, and gives his younger siblings their baths. Rosie is responsible for straightening up the shelf on the porch where we keep our shoes and (when she remembers) for feeding the dog. And Abe helps Zeke on garbage night, helps Rosie clean her room, and periodically goes through the yard picking up trash.

They work and we work because we, like Carol Channing, want the days of our lives to seem sunny as summer weather. So when there's housework to do, we make sure and do it together.

4. Breast Is Best

Once, when my son Abraham was six weeks old, I was standing in line at my local bakery. I had him in a sling, and I was feeding him. The sling's fabric was twisted and my hair was caught in the knot, but the baby had finally taken his bottle, and I was loath to adjust anything for fear of disturbing our tenuous peace. I rocked a bit on my heels. The baby paused in his sucking, and I held my breath.

Suddenly a voice behind me said, "You know, breast is best." I turned. The speaker, a woman a few years older than I, smiled pleasantly.

Now, the correct response to that comment might have been a stern rejoinder to mind her own business. It might even have included a series of expletives. Instead, what I did was burst into tears and launch into a long explanation about how the milk in the bottle was my own, pumped at four in the morning while everyone else in the house was asleep. I had in fact been pumping breast milk for Abraham every two hours, I told this stranger, because my son was born with a palate abnormality that made it impossible for him to suck properly from the breast.

Abe's feeding problem wasn't diagnosed until he was two weeks old. He weighed a healthy seven and a half pounds when he was born, a nice, plump baby. Immediately, however, he began losing weight, and by the time, ten days later, the pediatrician finally made time to see him, he was dangerously thin. No one, not the nurses in the hospital, nor the pediatrician who visited him there daily during the four days of my recuperation from my C-section, nor the hospital lactation consultant, nor even I, his mother, had noticed that the baby was getting no milk when he nursed. None of them had noticed his abnormal palate. He had probably not managed to extract more than a few ounces of milk a day since he was born, a tenth of what he should have been consuming. He was, in short, starving to death.

I had been worrying about the baby's weight from the day after he was born. For the first few days, after he nursed, my breasts would leak colostrum, the substance responsible for clearing the baby's bilirubin and meconium and passing on a jolt of immunoglobulins. Loath to waste the precious liquid, I'd asked for a breast pump. My plan had been to pump my breasts empty immediately after he nursed, and then mix the colostrum with a bottle of sugar water, which I would then encourage him to drink. The hospital lactation consultant had walked in on me. "Why are you doing that?" she'd said, pointing to the bottles hooked up to the pump. "You've got plenty of milk." I'd pumped for only a minute, but produced at least an ounce of colostrum. Instead of wondering why my breasts were still so full after the baby had supposedly nursed, she confiscated the pump.

For the next week or so, my brain still fogged by painkillers and sleep deprivation, I fretted. Whenever anyone came to see him, I would ask, "Do you think he looks too skinny?" When I changed his diaper, I would measure the circumference of his thigh with my thumb and middle finger. Again and again I asked Michael if he thought the baby was gaining weight as he should. When I couldn't get an appointment with the pediatrician, I asked the local public health nurse to come by and weigh him. Unfortunately, and for reasons I never understood, she was far more interested in screening me for domestic violence than in evaluating the baby. "He's fine," she said absently, ticking off an item from her checklist. "Has your husband physically assaulted you in the past thirty days?"

I was worried, but not sufficiently to take action. I accepted everyone's reassurances that Abraham was doing fine, that my concern was nothing more than a reflection of my own neuroses. What Jewish mother *doesn't* think her baby should eat more? I even went forward with Abe's bris, performed by a *moyel* who happened to be a pediatrician and who also missed the fact that the baby was slowly dying of dehydration. The red wine the *moyel* dripped into Abe's mouth might in fact have been the most liquid the baby consumed in a single sitting in the entire previous eight days of his life.

I was, however, sufficiently concerned not to be altogether surprised at our pediatrician's response when she finally put him on a scale. She disappeared from the room and returned with a bottle of formula. "Give this to him," she said. "*Now.*" Abe drank four ounces of formula in five minutes, astonishing for a baby his age. I sat there feeding him and weeping, horrified that I had allowed my baby to starve, sick at the thought that he'd been in pain. He had cried a lot during his first few days of life, doing what he could to let us know that he was hungry. After a while, however, he had stopped. He was a good baby, we told people. We hadn't realized until that moment that he had simply grown too weak to utter more than the smallest whimper.

The pediatrician told us that she would allow us to take him home for one night, but if we couldn't put half a pound on him by the next morning, she would have to admit him to the hospital. Twenty-four hours later, when she put him on the scale, he had gained almost a full pound. I had not slept for even a moment the night before. Instead, I'd held him in my hands all night long, watching his emaciated chest rise and fall. During those long hours the membrane between life and death seemed so very thin. He was tiny, a weightless bundle of sticks wrapped in translucent skin. I felt his heart beating and the blood flowing through his thread-thin veins. Every breath seemed like it could have been his last. As soon as he opened his mouth, I or Michael popped in the bottle. We kept feeding him long past when he was full, long after he wanted to go back to sleep. We unwrapped him from his blankets, tickled the soles of his feet, anything to keep him awake and drinking. I began pumping that night, for forty-five minutes out of every two hours, giving myself no more than an hour and a quarter rest between sessions.

All this I told the woman standing in line behind me at the café. I told her how I had weathered plugged ducts and breast infections; I showed her that the milk in that very bottle was colored a faint shade of purple, from the gentian violet I'd been applying to treat a brutal case of thrush. To establish my breast-feeding bona fides, I even told her how especially traumatizing my failure to feed this baby was, given that I'd successfully nursed three children, one for nearly three years.

She gave me absolution. I was doing great, she said. Keep it up. Because, you know, breast really is best.

Over the course of the next six months I continued my punishing pumping schedule. I gave over the actual feeding of the baby to Michael, who, with the help of a bottle designed for babies with cleft palates, managed to keep Abe steadily gaining weight. I enlisted the assistance of a team of lactation consultants, one of whom visited nearly every day to help me try to teach Abraham to nurse. Every few hours I settled into the glider rocker in the darkened room, a nursing pillow circling my waist, and tried to cajole Abraham into doing something more with my nipple than halfheartedly moving it around his mouth with his tongue.

In a final, doomed effort, I took him to Los Angeles to consult with the Lactation Institute, a place that promised me it could solve the problems of any "nursing pair" (that is, mother and baby). I had imagined a medical clinic with dozens of labs and consulting rooms, staffed by white-coated experts spouting the latest in breast-feeding medical research. What I got looked less like a doctor's office than like the headquarters of a Marxist student newspaper circa 1971. There were the usual frayed posters on the wall—War Is Not Healthy" et cetera, the usual pile of magazines with names like the *Vegan Quarterly*, the *Lesbian's Guide to Yoga*, the *Spelt-Lovers Review*, and the usual assortment of herbal teas and mismatched crockery mugs. The lactation consultants were just like the others I'd been working with. Warm and supportive, they mothered me in a pepper-and-salt-crew-cut, Teva-sandals kind of way.

Best of all, they were confident they could help. Showing me an oversized syringe attached to a long, thin silicone needle, they said, "You fill the syringe with breast milk. Then you put your finger in his mouth and slide the needle in alongside it. While he sucks on your finger, slowly, *slowly*, depress the plunger. Make sure that you go no faster than he can swallow."

Easy as pie. Except that it took a full twenty minutes to give him a single ounce. At the time, Abraham was consuming about thirty-six ounces of breast milk a day. At that rate twelve hours of my day would be devoted just to feeding him. And unlike giving him the bottle or breast-feeding, syringe feeding took two hands and full concentration. No multitasking was possible. And add to that the six hours a day I spent pumping.

"But I have three other children!" I wailed when I did the math. "When do I sleep?"

"Well," the lactation consultant said, giving my shoulders a squeeze, "it's really just a question of how committed you are. In a few months I'm sure he'll have learned how to do it on his own."

I packed up the baby and took him back to the airport. I pumped on the plane, crouched in the space between my seat and the one in front of me, the baby precariously balanced against the armrest. I resolutely ignored the people around me who stared, transfixed and horrified, as I struggled to produce a replacement for the bottle of breast milk I'd just spilled all over my baby and my lap when turbulence shook the silicone needle out of his mouth and sent the full syringe flying.

When I returned home, I laboriously instructed Michael in the new technique.

"If he stops sucking your finger, you back off on the plunger," I said. "That way he only gets milk when he sucks, like he would from a nipple."

Michael had by now stopped looking at the baby and the syringe. Instead, he was staring at me, his mouth gaping. "Are you *kidding* me?" he said finally.

"I know it's really time-consuming," I said.

"You could say that," he said.

"But it's really just a question of how committed we are."

"You know what?" Michael said. "It turns out we're not that committed." He threw the syringe and the pack of replacement silicone needles into the trash.

That night when the lactation consultant called to check up on our progress, Michael took the phone away from me.

"We're finished," he told the lactation consultant, who had

just communicated so effectively her disappointment in me. "Enough is enough."

I pumped for a month or two after that, until I'd stockpiled enough breast milk in the freezer to take the baby through his six-month birthday. Then I returned the pump to the rental center and called it quits.

For the next year, whenever I mixed up a bottle of formula for Abraham, I felt a sense of stabbing shame, shame I still feel, despite myself, to this day. In the park and at preschool, the other mothers—the *Good* Mothers—would cast a censorious glance at Abe's bottle and ostentatiously loose their pendulous breasts from their cow-spotted nursing bras. As they cuddled their expert nurser babies, I would blush. They, unlike me, were committed. I was a Bad Mother.

The reaction I had to having failed to nurse a baby whose malformed palate made it impossible was the same one I'd experienced after my attempt at a VBAC, five years before. That effort had resulted in forty-four hours of unmedicated labor, followed by another C-section. With Abraham, I immersed myself in the community, virtual and actual, of lactation consultants and La Leche groups, and when pregnant with his older brother, Zeke, I spent most of my time online, chatting and reading about how to avoid a medically unnecessary Cesarean. And all Cesareans were, at least according to the "experts" in natural childbirth populating the online VBAC communities, unnecessary. The women around me were having their babies in birthing tubs and presenting their midwives with eight-page, lavender-scented birth plans. Granted, I live in Berkeley, where the idea of an elective C-section is about as remote as a twenty-four-hour Rush Limbaugh marathon. Perhaps in other parts of the country a woman who ends up under the knife is not derided as "too posh to push." Posh or not, I never got to push. After forty-four hours a doctor shoved my midwife aside and, after asking me, "Are you *trying* to kill your baby?," ordered a C-section.

When Zeke was a fussy newborn who loathed all systems of transportation, especially his stroller, I was once walking home from running errands. I had been holding him all day, and my back felt like it had been worked over by a squad of foul-tempered ninjas wielding nunchakus. I put him in the stroller and began pushing as fast as I could in the direction of home. Hoping to distract him from the fact that he was separated from my body by a full foot and a half, I kept up a constant patter. On the final, uphill leg of the trip I said something like "Yes, yes, the world is a terrible place, and you are the saddest baby in it." A woman walking in front of me spun around, stopping in her path, her hand clutching her mouth in horror. "How dare you!" she said, lips white with rage. "How dare you impose your negative view of the universe on that child?"

I'm sure that there are women who circumcise their sons, who use disposable diapers, and who feed their infants formula who are smug, snarky, and unpleasant. But there seems to be a particular brand of sanctimony practiced by those who choose to exclusively breast-feed, use a family bed, and wear their babies in slings—choices generally associated with attachment parenting. Proponents of attachment parenting nurse their babies, wean them as late as possible, wear them in slings, co-sleep, and reject any discipline that is not "positive." There are eight principles of attachment parenting, developed by Dr. William Sears and his long-suffering wife, but they are, frankly, too dull to enumerate. Suffice it to say that I have been informed by at least one attachment-parenting adherent (and not as the punch line of a joke) that a baby's body should be in constant, *uninterrupted* contact with that of one of her parents for her entire first year of life. Anything less is child abuse.

Of course, the majority of devotees of Dr. Sears are marvelous, generous people whose sole interest lies in doing the best they can to raise contented, secure children. But why are there so many others who are so very self-righteous?

The twelve-thousand-member Berkeley Parents Network is an online community founded and directed by a woman named Ginger Ogle. The advice posts are some of the site's most popular—hundreds of people post every month seeking guidance on everything from potty training to how to deal with a philandering spouse. There are hot-button issues on the message board—moderators are warned that discussions of breast-feeding, co-sleeping, immunizations, spanking, stay-at-home moms, circumcision, and television have a history of generating "emotional responses." One issue in particular seems to draw out people's ire. In September 2003, in response to a desperate mother's plea for advice on how to sleep-train her wakeful baby, an anonymous poster referred to all non-Sears-sanctioned mothering styles as "Abandonment Parenting." Here was a mother driven to distraction by the fact that her baby had not allowed her more than a couple of hours of sleep in months, and her attempt to seek succor and support was greeted with an accusation of child neglect.

In a letter to subscribers, Ginger responded, "[W]e seem to have an ongoing problem on the newsletters with some of our attachment-parenting subscribers making the assumption that the rest of us have missed the boat and need to be instructed on the proper techniques of parenting—for whatever reason, it is not a problem we have on the newsletters with those who hold other views—just the attachment-parenting people." Things were quieter for a bit after Ginger's note, but soon enough the scolding resumed.

I have seen women on the sites (and it is *always* women) accusing one another of practicing "detachment parenting," of traumatizing their babies by allowing them to cry, of dooming their babies to lives of "insecurity and confidence problems." I've read posts that inform mothers who don't sleep with a copy of Dr. Sears's *Baby Book* tucked under their pillows that they will never have children who are as healthy, well developed, and independent as those lucky ones born in "non-Western" cultures. Your baby misses the womb, these women shrill. The first nine months of life should be considered the second stage of gestation! Don't put that baby down!

A woman named Julie, who writes a blog called A Little Pregnant about her struggles with infertility and the premature birth of her son, received a similar tongue-lashing when she posted about how her pediatrician had recommended a mild sleep-training regimen that included allowing the baby to cry for a short period. One reader told her that her son "feels abandoned and his primal instincts kick in for self-preservation (I'm alone in the world, I must conserve energy or die)." "On message boards I got called everything from negligent to monstrous," Julie told me. "I was accused of everything from lying about his neonatologist's advice to not loving the child I'd worked so hard to have."

When I asked Ginger Ogle why she thinks attachment-parenting adherents in particular can be so strident, she said she thinks it's because this kind of parenting is a belief system, nearly a religion. "Some of these parents sincerely believe in attachment parenting, homeopathy, cloth diapers, breast-feeding, baby wearing, not vaccinating, et cetera, in exactly the same way that Southern

Baptists sincerely believe in the death penalty, a strong military, the right to life, heterosexuality, and the Bible as the Word of God," Ogle said. While many baby wearers surely care little about what anyone else is doing, it is inarguable that certitude generally does not tolerate dissent. It responds to it with fury. Those of us whose parenting style can be described as "a series of reflexes, instincts, and minute-by-minute adjustments," as Julie of A Little Pregnant puts it, rather than as a philosophy, are less invested in our own practices. What we do is often less a matter of conviction than one of convenience. What we need to remember is that there is no need to apologize for that, even when confronted with the most red-faced outrage.

It's also important to acknowledge that the impulse to tsk-tsk has probably been indulged in, at one time or another, by all parents. I remember grocery shopping once, not long after my oldest child had been diagnosed with mercury poisoning as a result of eating no more than a single tuna salad sandwich a week. When I saw a pregnant woman tossing a few cans of tuna into her cart, I barreled over to her and launched into a diatribe during which the words "You really shouldn't" were repeated more than once. Only when I finally noticed that she was sidling away down the aisle did it dawn on me that, whatever my intentions, whatever the truth of my claim, I had no business giving a lecture to a total stranger.

What is it about parenting that allows us to indulge our inner scold? Normally most of us don't feel particularly threatened about the choices other people make. You live in a split-level ranch, I live in a Craftsman bungalow. I might like my house more than yours—I might even tell a friend I think your house is ugly—but I'd never stop you on the street and tell you to do something about your aluminum siding. Sure, each issue (even architecture) has its fanatics, but parenting seems to have more, and they're more vocal. Perhaps it's because there is so much at stake. Another parent's different approach raises the possibility that you've made a mistake with your child. We simply can't tolerate that, because we fear that any mistake, no matter how minor, could have devastating consequences. So we proclaim the superiority of our own choices. We've lost sight of the fact that people have preferences.

As a parent, I am absolutely certain of only one thing: my own fallibility. I used disposable diapers because it's easier. I circumcised my sons because we're Jewish (though I cried wretchedly through both ceremonies). I breast-fed my babies for as long as they would agree to it. I sleep-trained two of my children, Ferberizing one and Weissbluth-izing another. I feed my kids organic food and milk, but Abe consumes only two food groups—meat and candy. I wouldn't be surprised if he eats a pound of chocolate a week. My kids are not allowed to watch TV during the week, but on weekends even the little ones veg out to *The Simpsons*.

I have tried to learn to accept these "failures," to inure myself to those who are so confident that they do it all so much better than I do. But still, eleven years after my second C-section and five years after Abe's adventures in breast-feeding, there is a defensiveness about the way I tell those stories. I tried *really hard*, I seem to be saying. It's not my fault. Forgive me.

There is little I do as a mother that can't be criticized, not least by myself. Parenting is incredibly hard work, even without having to look over your shoulder to make sure you're doing it the way the neighbors (actual and cyber) think you should. Let's all commit ourselves to the basic civility of minding our own business. Failing that, let's just go back to a time when we were nasty and judgmental, but only behind one another's backs.

5. Tech Support

When I realized I was pregnant with Zeke, the first thing I did—even before making a doctor's appointment to verify the accuracy of the two pink lines—was join an online support group for pregnant women due in the month of June. It was back in the dark ages of 1997, and there were no Yahoo or Google groups. Hell, no one had even *heard* of Google. Those were the days when we relied on AltaVista and Ask Jeeves for navigation through the ether. People were only just beginning to talk about this thing called the World Wide Web, and we had yet to reap the benefit of 112 million blogs sharing information about the genesis of toenail fungus or whether Number Six is a figment of Gaius Baltar's imagination. Those were more innocent times, before the proliferation of mommy blogs and online parenting magazines, when BabyCenter was in its infancy and Anne Lamott still posted essays about her young son, Sam, on Salon's Mothers Who Think.

Most of my friends were not using e-mail as regularly as I was—probably because they had yet to quit their time-consuming and intellectually satisfying careers for the more mundane pleasure of killing time while the baby napped. But there was a group of us, thirteen women in all, some of whom I knew from college, others whom I had met at journalism school, who began a regular correspondence. I'm not going to share with you the humiliating name we gave ourselves, but suffice it to say that it was an era when the prefix "cyber" still had a cachet of cutting-edge and the literary genre of chick lit had not taken over the front tables of bookstores in swaths of Pepto-Bismol pink.

My online buddies were already regular e-mailers, sometimes shooting off as many as ten a day, but if you are a fast reader and suffer from graphomania, thirteen correspondents, no matter how prolific they are, are not enough to fill even a short nap. Also, although I could e-mail with those friends and talk to my live ones about what my toddler might have eaten to turn her shit that particular shade of Easter egg blue, none of them was pregnant, and, more important, none of them was due in *June*. I wanted companionship from women who were experiencing precisely the same quantity and quality of nausea and first-trimester narcolepsy as I was.

By the time I joined toward the end of my first month of pregnancy, the Listserv for expectant mothers due in June had at least fifty members. The group fluctuated in size over the course of that first trimester, increasing as more women discovered us and ebbing at the eight-week mark, when we had our first ultrasounds and some heartbeats failed to be detected. Members came from all over the English-speaking world, although most of us were American. The group included women of all economic classes: single mothers on welfare and the wives of investment bankers, waitresses and pediatric neurosurgeons. There was less in the way of racial diversity—with a few exceptions, the women were white—but in other ways we were as various a group as could be assembled from the multitude of women who got knocked up in September or October and also happened to own a computer with a decent modem.

Again with some exceptions, these were not women I was likely to come across in the course of my day-to-day life, which was then carried out on the playgrounds and in the Gymboree classes of West Los Angeles. There was the woman, for example, whose husband left her in the second month of her pregnancy, leaving her to raise all *five* of their children without any assistance, financial or emotional. There was the pediatric oncologist who left her practice upon becoming pregnant with her Junebug (yes, that's how we referred to our yet-to-be-born DDs and DSs—darling daughters and darling sons, for the uninitiated) and became the first (and surely most overqualified) lesbian Brownie troop leader in her housing development. There was the Internet entrepreneur supporting her agoraphobic DH—who by the time her Junebug could speak was neither her D nor her H. And there was my favorite, the polyamorous frequent poster, who never seemed to understand why the father of her baby and his other partner did not greet her pregnancy with as much joy as she did.

I enjoyed communicating with these strangers, even as they occasionally drove me nuts with their whining about hemorrhoids and breast tenderness. I was doing my own whining about hemorrhoids and breast tenderness, and they were the only people who were willing to "listen" to me without their eyes glazing over in a combination of tedium and disgust at my soul-crushing self-absorption. I found myself rapt by discussions about whether it's best to find out a baby's sex or wait and "be surprised,"* how much spotting was normal, whether a bassinet was a necessary item. I'm fully aware of how vacant and silly most of these conversations were, but pregnancy is, at least in my experience, a time when intellectual stimulation often takes a back seat to literal navel-gazing. When I was flush with the hormones of pregnancy or

*As if finding out your baby's gender is any less of a surprise at three months than at birth.

breast-feeding, far more of my free time was spent considering my condition and rubbing cocoa butter into my belly than engaging in any kind of productive behavior.

The members of the Junebug list were, by and large, sweet and supportive of one another. When the mother of five gave birth, we took up a collection for her; when someone shared bad news, we were always ready with sympathy. Most of us had yet to come across an Internet troll—there were fewer of them back then. But even in those halcyon early Internet days, we got into flame wars. They were over the usual subjects, familiar to any woman who has spent even an hour surfing the mommy Web. Breast-feeding versus bottle-feeding, cloth diapers versus disposable, the safety of anal sex during pregnancy (okay, that was just the polyamorous mom, although I'm willing to bet that there were many women with opinions on the issue who chose to maintain their dignity by not stating an official position). I tried not to start flame wars myself, but I have to admit that I was always the first to launch a spirited defense of a member who I believed was unjustly attacked.

Things never degenerated into true ugliness, however, because we were not anonymous. We used our real first names, and while it's possible that Julie or Joanne was really a troll named Philip wearing crusty boxer shorts and a coffee-spattered wife-beater, sitting hunched over his laptop in a cockroach-infested studio apartment in Van Nuys, and getting off on pretending to be a twenty-eight-year-old Mormon woman from Salt Lake expecting her third baby on June 14, it seemed unlikely. And even if there was such a troll, Philip (or Brian or Ahmed or whoever) was such a good actor and generally such a supportive correspondent that it didn't really matter if the Mormon mom was only a figment of his twisted imagination.

On the Junebug list, most of us got what we were looking for:

reassurance that we were normal, that we were doing things well enough, that we were—or were going to be—Good Mothers.

It was when I expanded my Web communities beyond this fairly personal list that the level of discourse deteriorated, and what support was on offer began slowly to be outweighed by a toxicity that seemed designed to destroy my sense of well-being rather than encourage it. Web sites like UrbanBaby and Berkeley Parents Network, while still providing plenty of useful tips on where to buy discount Robeez and what you should pay your babysitter, seem to degenerate with surprising frequency into full-pitched battles, the subtext of which is not only that we disagree but that your opinion, in its utter and fundamental wrongness, makes you the worst mother in the world. It is in the poisonous sludge of the comments sections that you see the worst in people.

During 2005 and 2006, I had a column on Salon.com in which I wrote about all sorts of subjects ranging from my mother's battles with Medicare, to the rights of juvenile defendants, to how much weight I gain every holiday season. I tried to be timely, and I tried to be honest, and I tried to write with humor about difficult subjects. By the time I'd published my second column, I had stopped looking at the comments. So many people wrote, and while many responses were complimentary or even just respectful in their disagreement, many others were laced with such venom, expressed such a loathing for absolutely everything about me, that I simply couldn't bear to read them anymore. For someone who writes memoir, I am unfortunately rather thin-skinned, and respond to most criticism—at least the personal kind—by falling into a pit of self-loathing. "She's right," I think. "I am that bad, and worse. Oh, my poor, poor children."

I've decided, in the interest of full disclosure, and because I am in the mood to indulge my masochistic streak, to include a few typical examples of the kind of response my columns received on Salon:

> "[Y]et another article that reinforces my impression that Ayelet Waldman is, in layman's terms, a FREAK. I hope Salon's remittance goes directly into some kind of trust fund to pay for her poor kid's future psychotherapy."

> "[P]leeeaassseee pleeeeeease take her awaaaaaaaaaaayyyyyyyyyyyyyyy: she's RUINED Michael Chabon for me. I'll never read another of his books, EVER. I won't be ABLE to—just THINKING of him married to HER makes me ILL."

> "I always need to take a shower after I read Ayelet Waldman's pieces."

Even the process of cutting and pasting those sentences makes me cringe, in spite of the fact that when they were written I was already no stranger to controversy, nor to hate mail. The essay I wrote about loving my husband more than my children, the one that made me the butt of such hysterical fury all over the Web, landed me on *Oprah*, where I faced down a studio full of wrathful mothers, with only the eponymous host at my side.* But being defended *only* by Oprah is like relying for nuclear deterrence *only* on the U.S. arsenal of nuclear warheads. You won't be surprised to learn that I won the daytime TV battle. By the end of the show all the angry mommies were reassuring Oprah that they agreed with me.

---

*There were a few mothers who were there to agree with me, and an expert on fatherhood, too, but somehow they paled in comparison to the woman who lunged across the stage screaming, "Let me at 'er!"

No, I was no neophyte to insult. I had been treated to plenty of rage and sanctimony—I live in *Berkeley* after all. But there is something special, having nothing to do with me in particular, about the kind of abuse people hurl at one another over the ether. It's ubiquitous, from the political Web sites where people attack even the most neutral of comments, to the vacuous echo chamber that is Gawker (and I say this even though they honored Michael and me with the title of third-most-annoying literary couple). It is a truism to point out that it is because of its anonymity that the Web has become a snark-filled cesspit. If the person who called me a freak had not been permitted the cloak of anonymity, I bet he would have figured out another way to state his objection. The folks who hawk phlegm in letters columns are always too cowardly to sign their real names.

Don't get me wrong, I love the Web. I revel in its breadth and depth of information. In the past twenty-four hours alone I have used the Web to look up the following pieces of information: the maximum speed of a classic single-hulled wooden schooner; current presidential polling figures for Colorado, Florida, Ohio, and Minnesota; how incomplete grades are awarded at Harvard College; who on my street gave the maximum donations to which presidential candidate; the hours of low tide in Blue Hill, Maine, on July 4 of last year; the square footage of the average boxing ring; the hours of operation of the Two Bird Café in San Geronimo; what percentage of Americans are idiotic enough to believe Barack Obama is a Muslim; the cost of custom-designed Vans; the winner of last year's National Book Award; the cost of a set of sails for the above-referenced schooner; which of Paganini's capriccios is more challenging to play, no. 5 or no. 24; the names of string quartets; the starting time of the movie *The Incredible Hulk* at my local cineplex; the relative merits of local Ethiopian restaurants; Golden

Gloves rules regarding the composition of boxing gloves; the average weight of five-year-old American boys and the correlation of emaciation with delayed cognitive development; the efficacy of Cetaphil as a remedy for lice infestation; whether frequent lice re-infestation has ever been used as a justifiable defense in a case of assault; the cost of a flight between Oakland, California, and New York City; the cost of a flight between New York City and Bangor, Maine; nutritional information on agave nectar; and the average number of puppies in a litter of dachshunds. (I fear that list may be incomplete.)

I have been involved in a myriad of Listservs and online communities—one for owners of Bernese mountain dogs, another for devotees of raw-meat dog food (I know, I know), a whole host of sites dealing with various aspects of the 2008 presidential elections. I have lurked on sites offering information on the treatment and care of children with ADHD, on up-to-the-minute information and photographs of women's high-heeled shoes, on the side effects of psychotropic medications, on writing, and skin care, and the proper treatment of plantar fasciitis. All of these get ugly, some with more regularity than others. But with the exception of the political Web sites, the vitriol is worst when the subject is motherhood. And even on political Web sites, the targets of the most venomous cyber-assaults are, I believe, more often women than men.

Periodically over the course of human history we come upon an intersection of technology and some long-dormant trait of human or animal behavior, some characteristic we would never have suspected without the arrival of an invention that unexpectedly reveals it. Dogs offer a perfect example. Humans worked to domesticate the descendants of wolves, creating over millennia a canine companion that can hunt, herd sheep, protect its human and his home, and guide the blind. Then, in 1903, the first Model A's rolled off Henry Ford's assembly line, and it suddenly became clear that the entire fifteen-thousand-year effort had served to create a creature perfectly suited to one activity: sticking its snout out the window of a car traveling down the interstate at sixty-five miles per hour.

It's the same with mothers and the Internet. When the ARPANET first came online, nobody in the Department of Defense had any idea that they were creating the most critical piece of the mommy war* puzzle. There have always been plenty of forums in which to make mothers feel insecure, but we have, with the creation of the Web and the proliferation of motherhood-related Web sites, reached some kind of nexus, a conjunction of maternal anxiety, misogyny, guilt, leisure, and technology that has been, on balance, a big bummer for contemporary mothers.

In 2006 the University of Maryland published a study that showed that women are twenty-five times more likely to be the targets of malicious online attacks than men. The Web doesn't just bring out the worst in all of us, it brings out the most misogyny, and the most self-loathing. Women have always been nasty to one another, but the Internet has widened the reach of each individual's venom. Where once you actually had to know someone to make her miserable (or at least know someone who knew someone), now you can spew bile on tens of thousands of strangers with a single click of the mouse. And it's not just the breadth of the effect; it is its depth, too. Because so much of the traffic on the Web is anonymous, we allow ourselves to sink to a level that would

---

*Yes, I know, I hate the term, too. It's usually used by people like Dr. Phil, because the image of professional women and stay-at-home mothers tearing out each other's throats spikes ratings, but I'm not using it like that. I'm just talking here about all the ways we mothers make one another feel like shit.

sicken us if we heard ourselves speaking out loud. Remember that Bad Mother police force? How many of those cops might have opted for early retirement if they were not able to sit around in their nightgowns in the middle of the night, slapping virtual cuffs on each other and sentencing strangers to the chair?

I am by no means ready to give up on the Web. I'm not going to go off and join a Luddite community of Wi-Fi-phobes deep in the Arizona desert. (Did you know that there are people who claim to be *allergic* to Wi-Fi?) I am not even ready to give up on joining online affinity groups of mothers. I made it through the bleak months of trying to get Abie to nurse in part because of the wisdom and support of the women of PumpMoms, who not only taught me how to get three letdowns in a single pumping session but also refrained from criticizing me when I decided that, with my nipples the size and shape of elderly ballpark franks and my baby thinking of me as merely that lady strapped to the bright yellow pumping machine on the other side of the room, it was time for me to quit.

I think the time is past when we can hope for a civil society to prevail on the Web. That genie is out of the bottle. The only thing we can do is try to remember that the Internet can be a pastry laced with poison, especially for mothers, and as we enjoy its many benefits, we must remind ourselves to take small bites. We can protect our kids with cyber-bullying statutes, but as far as their mothers are concerned, I fear we have no choice but *caveat prolaptor.* Let the surfer* beware.

---

*Technically, slip-and-slider, but it was as close as I could get.

6. Like a Fish Needs a Bicycle

number of years ago, Michael's cousin David was killed in an accident. He was commuting to work on his bicycle when he was hit by a car speeding through a turn. After he died, his wife, Ariel, told me that one of the many things she missed about him was having a man in the house to fix a dripping faucet, put together an Ikea cabinet, change the batteries in the smoke detector. David was killed the day before trash pickup, and that night the cans did not go out. The next week, as Ariel hauled out the heavy bins brimming with the detritus of a week's shiva—paper plates, plastic cups, uncountable wads of damp tissue—she realized that she was alone.

There was nothing traditional about those two. David was like Michael, as involved a father as I've ever seen. He didn't just change the occasional diaper; he assumed equal responsibility for the care of their daughter. Ariel is a massage therapist, a doula, and while I'm not sure, I'm willing to bet she'd call herself a feminist. Still, when it came to home repair, the division of labor fell along traditional lines. That's the way it is in my marriage, too.

For all my adamant feminism, it never occurred to me to take Michael's name when we married, and not just because to do so would have horrified my mother. I am a supporter of abortion rights, of equal pay for equal work, of the rights of women prisoners, of all the time-honored feminist causes, and then some. During the periods in my marriage when I chose to stay home with my kids, even though I knew I was contributing to our family by caring for our children, I still felt that my worth was less because I wasn't earning.

Even given all this, I haven't changed a lightbulb in sixteen years, since the day I met my husband.

Before I was married, I didn't consider my failure to manage even basic hand tools a feminist inadequacy. I thought it had more to do with being Jewish. The Jews I knew growing up didn't do "do-it-yourself." When my father needed to hammer something, he generally used his shoe, and the only real tool he owned was a pair of needle-nose pliers. My non-Jewish friends had fathers who changed faucet washers (they knew what faucet washers *were*) and re-planed sticky doors. My father hacked with a pair of needle-nose pliers at anything my mother was not willing to call a repairman to fix.

Now when something breaks in the house, I respond with the panic of my forebears. Every popped lightbulb is a catastrophe, every leaky faucet spells, if not the end of the world, then surely the beginning of months of crack-assed plumbers hunched over my sinks and toilets, flushing my hard-earned dollars down their mysterious drains. It always takes me a minute to remember that Michael is not like my father. He's got a set of needle-nose pliers, even two, but he's also got slip-joint pliers and groove-joint pliers and pliers I don't even know the names of. When the faucet leaks, he not only knows what a washer is, he can replace it. Moreover, he enjoys the job. He hangs pictures, he unclogs toilets, he knows what to do when the computer flashes that scary little bomb icon.

Each time, after my initial moment of hysteria, I feel a wave of contentment, of security. I feel protected. I am a damsel in clogged-drain distress, and he is my knight with shining plunger.

It is uncomfortable for me to admit that when it comes to this part of our lives, I want to feel sheltered and cared for. There is something seductive about letting go of this area of concern. Instead of causing anxiety, a dripping faucet now reminds me that there is someone in my life who can take care of such things.

When Michael goes away, I allow things in the house to fall into a state of ridiculous disarray. I avert my eyes from the blinking oil light in the car; I prop a door closed with a chair until he comes home to fix the latch. I lie in the dark and listen to the toilets running, waiting for him to do whatever it is he does to make them quiet again. As lightbulbs burn out, the kids and I just squint in the ever-increasing gloom.

When I was single and lived alone, I was perfectly capable of getting the ladder out and changing bulbs on my own. So what is it about marriage that has made me so dependent, and why, even witnessing the warning of Ariel's example, do I continue to allow myself to behave like some helpless 1950s sitcom wife?

Now that I am working again, this is the *only* area of our lives where traditional roles hold us in such sway. Otherwise, as I've told you before, our partnership is remarkably equal. Michael does as much or more of the actual floor time of parenting. He cleans more than I do. He does all the cooking. Given this, and given that I am someone who takes equality between the sexes so seriously, shouldn't the fact that I seem to enjoy a certain kind of helplessness bother me? Feminism, for all that the word has fallen out of fashion, is ubiquitous enough that it feels vaguely shameful for a woman to want to feel protected. A *good* feminist mother would be able to do it all—assemble the crib, prepare her own organic baby food, snake the drain, breast-feed the baby, and regrout the bathtub.

What I feel worst about is that I am perpetuating this dichotomy into the next generation. Michael is training our sons to follow in his competent footsteps, but not, alas, our daughters. It's not that he doesn't want to teach the girls. Every time he busts out his electric screwdriver, he tries to recruit an assistant, but the only volunteers for the job in our house are male. The girls would rather stick to building elaborate fairy houses for their tiny Japanese rubber hamsters or running up leg warmers on their sewing machine, and I never try very hard to convince them to drop everything and hold the clamp for Daddy while the wood glue dries. A Good Mother, one who took seriously her obligation to prepare her daughters for an egalitarian world, would be cracking the home-repair whip, wouldn't she?

Michael feels no counterpoint to my feminist crisis. I am solely responsible for our finances, a job that, while many women do it, might be considered the traditional purview of a man. Yet he doesn't find it emasculating that he hasn't paid a bill in as long as I haven't changed a lightbulb. On the contrary, he's relieved.

Perhaps my lack of concern with my home-repair incompetence is nothing more than a vestige of that patriarchy I spent so much time reading about and demonstrating against in college. Maybe I'm not as much of a feminist as I think I am. After all, I stopped working and stayed home with kids for years, and neither Michael nor I even considered for a moment the possibility that he would stop writing. Maybe I enjoy feeling inept with a hammer and a screwdriver because part of me thinks that's how girls are supposed to behave. Maybe that's why I haven't been more aggressive about making my daughters learn the intricacies of the toilet's balky flushing mechanism.

But I don't think so.

I think this has more to do with the nature of marriage. In every union roles are assumed, some traditional, some not. Michael used to pay his own bills; I used to call my own repairman. But as marriages progress, you surrender areas of your own competence, often without even knowing it. You do this in part because it's more efficient for each individual to have his or her own area of expertise, but also as a kind of optimistic gesture. By surrendering certain skills, you are affirming your belief that the other person will remain there to care for you in that way.

This kind of capitulation is not without its pitfalls, of course. Every woman who has given over the financial reins only to find herself divorced and penniless knows its dangers. Still, one of the wonderful things about an intimate partnership is the division of life, the parsing out and sharing of responsibility.

One of the tragedies of a lost love is the collapse of this system, and the confrontation of the ways we've allowed ourselves to become dependent. When I think of Ariel alone in her house, learning for herself the things that she once relied on David for, my heart breaks. Ariel is a strong and able woman. Of course she can put together a cabinet or unplug a toilet. So could I, if I set my mind to it, and checked out a few books on home repair from the library. My heart breaks because this enforced proficiency is symbolic of David's absence, of all the ways in which she and her daughter must do without the man on whom they would still rely if only fortunes were different, if only that driver had taken the corner more slowly.

I suppose you could argue that this is precisely why we shouldn't give in to this seductive loss of expertise. You could even argue that we could view the end of a relationship as an opportunity to become stronger, to relearn or learn new skills. I don't know. I do know that I am not going to be picking up a hand tool anytime soon. I will continue to pay the bills; Michael will unclog the toilets. That is the way our marriage works; that is the bargain we struck without a word. My only wish is that I could take a page out of his book and refrain from feeling guilty about it.

7. My Mother-in-Law, Myself

When Zeke was in preschool, he came home every day and headed straight for the couch. He pulled me down next to him and cleaved his plump body to my own less adorably rotund one. He pressed his soft lips to my neck, nuzzling under my chin, breathing deep, as if he wanted to inhale every molecule of the fragrance he had missed in the four hours of our separation. He placed his palms on my cheeks and kissed me on the lips, languidly yet gravely, like a very small, round-cheeked lover.

I can't say that while he was gone, I missed him as much as he missed me; I did not prove my devotion by spending our time apart dripping tears onto the sand table and rocking in misery on the cushions of the book nook. I was too busy reveling in my time alone, getting my work done, going for solitary walks, reintroducing myself to my husband. But when Zeke returned, I leaped onto the couch with as much eagerness as he. Holding his fleshy, silky body was the most satisfying tactile experience I have ever had in my life. The flawlessness of an infant's skin is a trite metaphor, but his baby skin was even more buttery than most. And I'm not a child-aggrandizing mother blinded by love. I have four children, and this boy's skin was different. It felt like the freshest heavy cream tastes: smooth and round, fat and thick on the tongue. His body, too, was different. It's a wonder how what can inspire such disgust on an adult can be so delectable on an infant. Zeke is eleven years old now, as thin and wiry as a half-starved whippet, but when I close my eyes, I can still feel the give of his plump baby flesh under my fingers.

Once, when he was about four years old, while we were driving over the hill leading to our house, we passed the bright purple house that had always been his older sister's favorite.

"That's where we'll live when I grow up," Zeke said.

"Who? You and the person you marry?" Note that I didn't say "wife." Those of us who raise our families in Berkeley would never make assumptions about our children's sexual orientation.

"No. You and me."

"Aren't you going to get married and have children?" I asked, hearing to my horror a hint of the whine of my foremothers. You can take the babushka off the Jewish mother and dress her up in a pair of Seven for All Mankind jeans and Marc Jacobs Mary Janes, but she's still going to expect a passel of grandkids.

"My wife will sleep on the first floor with Daddy. You and I will live on the top floor. Together."

It's possible that a psychologically sound mother, a mother whose role model isn't the floating maternal head in Woody Allen's "Oedipus Wrecks," would not have been quite so pleased. Certainly a better mother would not have congratulated her son on such a fine plan and offered to cover half the mortgage.

Even now, although Zeke's pride does not allow him to linger in my arms for much longer than a minute or so, he still calls for me to lie with him at night; until he was seven, he still gave me "movie kisses"—kisses that last for a little longer than usual and involve a lot of twisting of the head and moaning. He still cuddles up to me, pressing his needle chin and knobby knees into me before spinning off to pick up his skateboard or go to the computer. And although he no longer plans to exile his wife to the far reaches of the lower floors of the purple house, neither is he particularly anxious to consider a life with a woman other than his mother.

I do not envy this phantom daughter-in-law of mine. I pity the young woman who will attempt to insinuate herself between my mama's boy and me. I sympathize with the monumental nature of her task. It will take a crowbar, two bulldozers, and half a dozen Molotov cocktails to pry my Oedipus and me loose from each other. She'd be better off turning her attention to decorating that downstairs in-law unit.

I sympathize with how much work she faces, but not with *her*. In fact, the very thought of this person, imaginary though she is, sends me into paroxysms of a kind of envy that is uncomfortable to admit. I make jokes about how I hope Zeke is gay so that he will bring home a lovely young man, rather than a nubile young girl who will cast a disparaging and dismissive eye on my crow's-feet and thick waist. This young man would be my friend. My ally even. In the more likely but far less appealing scenario, Zeke and his wife will screen their calls and roll their eyes as I leave increasingly frantic voice-mail messages. She will perfect an impression of me, complete with nasal whine and pinched lips, while he winces at the droll accuracy and drags her off to the bedroom while my forlorn voice begs to the empty air, "Please, darling, give your mother a call, just so that I know you're all right."

You'd think this obsessive love my son and I share would give me sympathy for my own mother-in-law. My mother-in-law and I are, in many ways, perfectly matched. Like me, she is an attorney. Like her, I am an eclectic and voracious reader. Both my mother-in-law and I are far too attracted to stories of personal and medical misfortune, and we enjoy recounting them with exquisite detail. We share the rather unattractive qualities of being both nosy and snoopy. These are not identical traits—the first indicates that we're interested in other people's doings and the second that we are not above making inquiries, subtle or not. A nosy person listens closely to a friend's confidences about her husband's sexual dysfunction, and maybe asks a prying question or two. A snoopy person combs through a friend's medicine cabinet looking for Viagra.

We should have gotten along famously, from the very first moment. And in a sense, we did. We could kill an hour with relative ease. Michael's eyes would glaze over early in the conversation, but I was always willing to egg her on.

"Was it more like an orange or a grapefruit? Did they get it all?"

"Can't he get his wages garnished for that?"

"How did she even know to get herself tested for chlamydia?"

We share these traits, and I should have had empathy for her. After all, she had experienced what I knew I would eventually: being the first love of your son and then watching helplessly as that devotion shifted.

But I found myself without compassion. On the contrary, I couldn't help but feel that my job was to step between her and her son. I cannot trace my attitude to any flaw in my mother-in-law. She is not domineering or overbearing, nor does she treat my husband as a prince around whom she flutters in constant and obsequious attendance. She is a calm and pleasant woman, unassuming and benign. Our first meeting augured well. We spent an entire weekend together in a small hotel suite. Michael brought me to Washington, D.C., where she was working on assignment for a month, so that I could meet her. Michael and I slept on a pullout sofa, separated from her by tissue-paper-thin walls. We had not been together very long, Michael and I, only a couple of months, and we were in the throes of that first hysteria of sexual infatuation where your body is attuned to your lover's every breath, and passing a night without proving that to each other is impossible to imagine.

My mother-in-law gamely ignored us. At meals, she kept her eyes on her menu while we snuggled on the other side of the table. She accompanied us on our visits to friends, walks through the city, nostalgic forays to the neighborhood where she had raised her son, the man I knew even then that I would marry, and never once behaved as I would have, if it had been Zeke canoodling with his girlfriend in the backseat of the car while I tried to point out how big the trees had grown in the yard of our old house. Not only did my mother-in-law tolerate what can only have been highly irritating behavior, but she actually seemed to enjoy our company.

Despite her fondness for gossip, Michael's mother is a reserved, quiet woman, the polar opposite of me in this regard. If, as Michael is fond of saying, my autobiography would be titled *Me and My Big Mouth*, hers would be called *Quiet, I'm Reading*. She is as restrained physically as she is verbally.

The next time we saw each other, at her house, she put her hand on my shoulder while placing a bowl of broccoli on the table. That instant of contact had Michael waxing rhapsodic for hours.

"She's never just spontaneously embraced one of my girlfriends like that," he said, his voice hushed with awe.

"Embraced?" I replied, genuinely confused. "When did she embrace me?"

"At the table. She hugged you at the table."

"You mean that time she sort of bumped into me?"

She's a little looser nowadays, and we hug and kiss easily when we meet after an absence, but she is by no means physically effusive. What felt to me like cool friendliness at the time was warmth to her; what felt to me like an accidental brush of her arm was to her a sign of something special.

None of which explains why, not long after that meal, when Michael and I moved to within half an hour's drive of my mother-in-law, I began to feel an intense sense of competition. I was jealous of her. The idea to move to the same part of the country was mine—I had a new job that took us there—but something about the proximity made me anxious. It brought forth a jealousy that might otherwise have simmered barely noticed, under the surface. I fear that I generated this on my own, entirely within my own head. My mother-in-law had, after all, been through this before; I am my husband's second wife, and the last in a long line of girlfriends. She must have been resigned to her fate as perennially second in his heart.

From early on, I felt deeply territorial about Michael and approached our relationship with a kind of ravenous intensity. When we first met, Michael and I told each other about our previous relationships. We traded details, laughed over them, shared our inside jokes with each other. I think I felt that only if I could insert myself into his history, consume it, if you will, could I assert the primacy of our relationship over all those prior ones. If I knew as much as he did about those women, especially his ex-wife, I could be secure.

Michael also told me about his childhood, as much as he remembered. I think much of my jealousy of my mother-in-law sprang from my belief that there were long years of his life that belonged exclusively to her, that lived only in her own memory. Those were years, I imagined, when she was the sun around which his little-boy self revolved. I could never own those years the way I tried to own the other epochs and loves in his history.

In thinking about my husband's relationship with his mother, I wonder if the very thing that should have given me the most peace of mind was what caused me the most consternation. There was none of the Sturm und Drang I was used to from my own family. His family seemed genuinely to enjoy each other's company, but not to be overly involved with one another. There was no bickering, no unrealistic demands, no slammed phones, no waves of passion and rage. They were *easy* with one another—mild even. They were the very opposite of Woody Allen and his mother's floating head. I was confused by it. It was so unlike anything I understood a mother-child bond to be. I, who called my mother three times a day, just didn't *get* that Michael and his mother could love each other without being overly entangled.

At the same time, I failed to be comforted by the fact that he made a deliberate choice to be with a woman whose temperament, unlike his mother's placidity, runs to extremes of passion and mood. You'd think these very differences would have made me more confident in my primary place in my husband's heart. You'd be wrong.

This tug-of-war between a mother and a daughter-in-law over a man is an age-old phenomenon, the stuff of sitcom jokes and Greek tragedy. Two women, decades apart, vying over the favors of a man who most often doesn't even know a battle is being fought. It's easy to imagine why women who define themselves through the status of the men in their lives and the attention those men pay to them would end up in competition. But my mother-in-law and I are not women like that. We are both women who pride ourselves on our independence, our careers. Even in the absence of an overbearing and territorial counterpart, I slipped into the combative role so easily, as if it were an inevitable part of being a woman marrying a man. It was as though the need to be the one, the *only*, in his life overcame even the most common of sense.

My campaign was subtle, and at the time I didn't even realize what I was doing. I insinuated myself between them delicately but decisively. I began complaining about my mother-in-law, and my primary target was her reserve. "How can you stand such diffidence?" I kept asking Michael. "Doesn't it drive you crazy?" Through cues as understated as holding his hand when we were together, I tried to make my primacy known. Michael and I were planning and paying for our own wedding, and we limited the guest list to our families and our own friends, effectively making my mother-in-law—and, by necessity of fairness, my own parents—mere invited guests at their own children's wedding.

When Michael and I spent time with my mother-in-law, I found myself using the first-person plural, an exclusionary tense if ever there was one. "We loved that movie," I would say. Or, "That's our very favorite restaurant, we'll take you next time we go." All this by way of showing her that he and I were a unit, a couple. *The* couple.

I even resented the weekly lunch date Michael and his mother shared. I had the grace to be ashamed of this resentment and tried to hide it, but I must have failed dismally, because over the course of our first few months together those lunches gradually ceased. Then I thought she barely noticed that they no longer lunched together, or didn't care, but in retrospect I think she just kept her feelings to herself.

My mother-in-law's style is much more subtle than my own. Because of her natural reserve, she would never have mentioned our rivalry, and it's even possible that she didn't feel it. Or at least wouldn't acknowledge the feeling. But it was there, lurking under the surface of even our most positive of interactions.

Michael, like most husbands in so many of this most stereotypical of domestic dramas, did his best to keep everyone happy, but

I think the primary emotion he experienced was confusion. After all, it was clear to him. I was his beloved. She was his mother. Two relationships entirely different one from the other.

I think he probably wished I'd just give it a rest.

And so this undercurrent of tension remained, with me grudging the time we spent with my mother-in-law, suggesting, for example, that Michael and I have a private Thanksgiving dinner in a beautiful lodge in the mountains, instead of with his family.

Then we had children, and something began to change. It was a gradual shift, one that took a while even to notice. But when I became the mother of Michael's children, I began, almost imperceptibly at first, to relax. Suddenly there could be no question that we, my children and I, were the primary family unit in Michael's life. It was as if once it became obvious that the competition was over, I could take my mother-in-law into my heart with all the grace of a good winner. Somehow, effortlessly, all the antagonism of our relationship simply evaporated. Once I was absolutely sure of my ascension and her usurpation, I could give in and become her friend.

A couple of years ago I invited my mother-in-law on our yearly family vacation. The invitation was a selfish one. With four children, the hotel would not allow us to cram into a single bungalow, and if we didn't bring a third adult, Michael and I would be forced to spend our vacation in separate rooms. I invited her as a glorified nanny. Within hours it became clear that she was much more than a third pair of hands.

Travel with four small children had always been gratifying in its way, but so, too, it had been a special kind of misery, with anxiety, squabbling, and lots of vomit. This time, while one child threw up in my lap, another ran down the airplane aisle to the bathroom, and two more catapulted out of their seats in a shrieking wrestling match, my mother-in-law kept her cool. She always keeps her cool. That's who she is. She can sometimes be stern, but she never loses control. What was miraculous was that when she was there, neither did I.

I went from resenting my mother-in-law to accepting her and finally to appreciating her. What appeared when I was first married to be her diffidence, I now value as serenity. The capacity for extravagant emotion that Michael finds so attractive in me can be exhausting, especially to a child. My moods are mercurial, and this can be terrifying. I know, because I was a daughter of a mother with a changeable temperament. My mother-in-law's mood is always consistent. She is the opposite of capricious. She is the most reliably steady person I have ever known.

Once, I chafed at any hour Michael spent with his mother, somehow viewing it as time stolen from me. Now I don't mind. They take our oldest daughter to musicals, an entertainment I find tedious in the extreme, or Michael takes all four of the kids to his mother's house for dinner when I am out of town. But my mother-in-law and I are far more likely to go out alone than the two of them are. We go shopping; we go to the movies. I enjoy spending time with her. She's a good companion, part friend, part mother. When Michael is out of town, she comes over for dinner, and just having her in the house eases me. She eases all of us.

That February, in Hawaii, my mother-in-law and I sat side by side under a tree on matching lounge chairs. Michael was in the water with the older children, and the little ones were playing in the sand next to us. My mother-in-law and I had each just finished the novels we were reading and had swapped, something I can rarely do with my husband, because he is a slow and methodical reader and because he is most often immersed in something like a thirteen-hundred-page annotated volume of Sherlock Holmes short stories or Gnome Press's *Porcelain Magician* by Frank Owen. My mother-in-law can be relied upon to have the new Philip Roth or Lorrie Moore. I remember looking out at Michael diving smoothly under the waves, and at the sun-kissed faces of my two youngest towheads as they dumped sand on their grandmother's feet. In the moment of quiet before the baby walloped his older sister on the head with his shovel and she kicked him over in the sand, I thought to myself, "This is nice." Then pandemonium broke out, and there were tears to dry and egos to soothe.

After we had finally managed to calm things down, my mother-in-law held Rosie on her lap, and I held baby Abie. He snuggled against me, his velvet cheek rubbing my chest. He smelled deliciously of coconut sunscreen and the strawberries he'd eaten for breakfast, and I breathed deep of his marvelous fragrance. He was just under a year old and had only two words reliably in his vocabulary, but one of them was "Mama." When he said my name, I kissed him, rubbing my lips against his soft, rubbery mouth and tickling his sun-warmed belly. I looked over at my mother-in-law. She returned my gaze with a complicated one of her own. I could tell that the sight of her baby grandson lolling on his mother's lap under a palm tree in the dappled Hawaiian shade pleased her. I wonder, though, if something else wasn't giving her just the tiniest bit of satisfaction. The prospect that one day I was going to do battle with this boy's wife, just as I had done battle with her. And I was going to lose.

8. Drawing a Line

I t was the night we wove an Iroquois cradleboard out of natural fibrous materials that drove me over the edge. It was 9:00 p.m., an hour *after* bedtime, when Sophie—eleven years old at the time—suddenly remembered that in addition to a written report, her Native American history assignment required a visual presentation.

"It's okay, I can do it," she said. "I just need some hemp."

Frankly, so did I.

I hate homework. I hate it more now than I did when I was the one lugging textbooks and binders back and forth to and from school. The hours my children spend seated at the kitchen table, their books spread out before them, the crumbs of their after-school snack littering the table, are without a doubt the worst of my day. If their teachers, delightful and intelligent people every one, were to walk through my kitchen door between 3:30 and 4:30 p.m. on a weekday, I could not guarantee their safety.

When Zeke was eight, he routinely had an hour of homework a night. Zeke is an interesting, creative kid, one who's described as having a lot of "personality." He's the kind of kid who, left to his own devices, thinks it's funny to write "a Rottweiler" as the answer to every question on the homework page, even the math problems. Especially the math problems.

Accordingly, either Michael or I have to sit next to him and insist that he read the directions in his homework packet, instead of riffing on the crazy soundtrack that runs in his head.

School for Zeke has always been work, and by the end of a seven-hour workday he's exhausted. But like a worker on a double shift, he has to keep going. When, halfway through kindergarten, we had to break it to him that this wasn't a one-year gig, that in fact he was looking at, conservatively, sixteen and a half more years of school, the expression on his face was one of deep, existential despair. That evening he calculated that the next time he could count on being really, truly happy was in sixty years, when he retires. His sister, however, is one of those cheerful Pollyanna types who finish their summer reading list before Memorial Day, and at eleven was already counting on getting at least one graduate degree. But even she hates homework.

When I sent out a feeler to mothers of other elementary-school students asking for their experiences with homework, my in-box was immediately flooded with replies, some furious, some rueful. "We had to set up an interview with someone in the community, transport the children, supervise the interview, take notes, take photos, print the photos, assist the students in making note cards for a speech, and help the kids make a poster about the community member," said Martha, the mother of twins in the Bay Area. Sounds like a nice project, doesn't it? It might have been—for a ten-year-old. But Martha's boys were in *second* grade.

Six-year-old Katie Williams of Maryland spent days trolling newspapers looking for "io" and "ou" configurations in order to begin her "Rainbow Words" assignment. "Do you know how many thousands of words we had to read to come up with enough to satisfy that assignment?" asks her mother. Once she found the words, Katie had to write each one over and over again, using every color of the rainbow. Get it? Rainbow words. Whatever happened to using a No. 2 pencil?

Another mother described the weekly timed math tests mandated by her kids' teacher. "Sixty problems correctly answered in four minutes. We parents are supposed to stand over our kids with stopwatches. My children are very different from each other, but they have this in common—they have both been in tears due to their fear of failing these inane tests. Mind you, these children are seven years old."

But my favorite is Carlie Williams's nephew. Assigned to construct a relief map of one of the fifty states out of plaster of Paris, the boy chose Nebraska. He made a flat rectangle. As his aunt said, "You've got to love a kid who puts into the assignment exactly the effort it's worth."

How would we be spending our time if we didn't have to slave over these piles of mind-numbing make-work? Maybe some kids would be vegging out in front of the television or exercising their thumbs on their Game Boys, but I would guess that's not what would be going on in my house, or in most others. Instead, we'd do the things we rarely have time for during the week, like go for bike rides or shoot hoops. My kids might even occasionally enjoy the opportunity to be bored. You remember boredom, don't you? That state where the imagination is forced to take over and create entertainment?

Harris M. Cooper, formerly the director of the Program in Education at Duke University and author of *The Battle over Homework: Common Ground for Administrators, Teachers, and Parents*, tells me that the homework load for most students has actually remained steady for the past fifty years, except for the group in which I did my very unscientific survey—middle- to upper-middle-class students in the lowest grades. Cooper says that because educators of middle- and upper-class children feel a great deal of pressure to maintain test scores, they up the homework ante.

I also learned from Professor Cooper—a.k.a. the homework guru—that there is *no* correlation between how much homework young children do and how well they comprehend material or perform on tests. Why? For a number of reasons. First, because their attention spans are just too short—they can't tune out external stimuli to focus on material. Second, younger children cannot tell the difference between the hard stuff and the easy stuff. They'll spend fifteen minutes beating their heads against a difficult problem, and leave themselves no time to copy their spelling words. Finally, young children do not know how to self-test. They haven't the faintest idea when they're making mistakes, so in the end they don't actually learn the correct answers. It isn't until middle school and high school that the relationship between homework and school achievement becomes apparent.

So why the hell did Zeke and I have to spend every afternoon of third grade gnashing our teeth over the commutative and associative properties of numbers when we could be playing catch?

The reasons, Cooper says, extend beyond Zeke's achievement in that particular grade. Apparently, by slaving over homework with my son, I am expressing to him how important school is. (Of course, this rationale assumes that I'm not also expressing audible rage at his teacher, or muttering curses about the authors of his math textbook.) When younger kids are given homework, Cooper says, it can also help them understand that all environments are learning ones, not just the classroom. For example, by helping calculate the cost of items on a trip to the grocery store, they can learn about math. The problem is, none of my children's assignments have this real-world, enjoyable feel to them. My children have never been assigned Cooper's favorite reading task—the back of the Rice Krispies box. Instead, we're up all night weaving hemp.

The final, and perhaps most important, reason to assign homework to young children, says Cooper, is to help them develop study habits and time-management skills that they'll need to succeed later in their academic careers. If you wait until middle school to teach them these skills, they'll be behind. I suppose this makes sense. Spending their afternoons slaving over trigonometry and physics will come as no surprise to my kids. By the time they're in high school, they won't even remember what it's like to spend an idle afternoon.

According to Cooper, all three of these rationales are based on the idea of keeping homework simple and short, and gradually building on its amount and complexity. The guideline educators typically use is the ten-minute rule. Children should be assigned ten minutes of homework per grade per night, starting in first grade. So how about kindergarten? Well, Cooper's a circumspect kind of guy, so he wouldn't condemn it outright, but he did say this: "At this age, kids should not be expected to do much on their own."

And what about those long-term homework projects that involve a lot of "integration of skills"—that favorite phrase I've heard again and again in all my children's classrooms? When used in younger grades, the lesson those projects often teach is, "When the going gets tough, Mom gets going," says Cooper. "Complex projects should probably not happen in the lower grades, and when they do, there should be clear expectations about parental involvement." Amen to that, I say, because otherwise the only skills being integrated are those of procrastination and panic, and those are plenty finely honed around our house by now.

Take heart, parents, and bring the quotations from the homework guru to your children's teachers. I did. When I e-mailed Zeke's third-grade teacher to say he was too loaded down with busywork, she agreed and said he shouldn't do more than half an hour of homework every night. She instructed me to draw a line at the bottom of the page once we've both had enough, no matter where he was on the assignment.

On the first day of the new regimen, after soccer practice, we set out his homework on the kitchen table. A page of spelling, two of math, a sheet of cursive. We got through the math okay, with me trying to hide the fact that I had to count on my fingers to check his work. He labored over the cursive, making rows of perfect *u*'s and *w*'s, the tips of his fingers white on the pencil, his tongue sticking out the side of his mouth. Then it was on to spelling. We made it almost to the end of the page, to the paragraph full of errors to correct. He made his proofreading marks, and as he got ready to copy out the corrected paragraph, I looked up at the clock. It had been forty minutes.

"That's enough, buddy," I said. "You did a great job." And I drew a line.

9. So Ready to Be the Mother of a Loser

A few years ago, Sophie and Zeke came home from school abuzz over the new game they'd learned in gym class. I'd never heard them express any kind of excitement about PE before—they are not natural athletes—but there they were strategizing and recounting the high points of their respective matches with unprecedented zeal. I tried to follow the discussion, but it was making little sense to me. My one foray into organized sports was a single spring on the Brookwell Cleaners softball team in sixth grade. I remember very little about the season other than the ache in my shoulder from holding my hand above my head in a futile attempt to distract the gnats from my face, the sound of my own teammates' jeers as I made my regular strikeout, and the euphoria of being allowed to take the bench whenever our team had the slightest chance of winning.

The game my kids were so agog over wasn't softball, though. It wasn't even foursquare, a game they'd once tried to explain to me without much success. Finally, I asked them what they were talking about.

"Dodgeball!" Zeke, then seven years old, announced gleefully. "It's really fun."

Dodgeball? My children were playing *dodgeball*? That cruel, brutal, violent school-yard game so mercilessly satirized in the 2004 film with Ben Stiller? The game, more importantly, that exemplified everything that was wrong with my childhood in suburban New Jersey, a short, pasty-faced Jewish girl in a town full of scrubbed blond athletes, their long tanned limbs toned from years of tennis lessons and country-club swim teams? Dodgeball? Over my dead body.

I know it's fashionable to claim to have been a nerd as a child, to insist on having scrabbled to hold on to the lowest tier of the social ladder, to recount years of torture at the hands of the golden and anointed. Trust me, I know just how trite my history of exclusion is. I know that when compared with a lifetime of true deprivation and abuse, suburban misery counts for little. Nonetheless, as someone who still, at forty-three, gets a clutch of nausea every time she drives by George Washington Junior High School, I am just not willing to let go of the reins of this particular hobbyhorse. I am convinced that my entire personality was formed in those long tile hallways where I was a victim of that most banal of childhood torments—ostracism. Everything can be explained by, every torque and twist in my character can be attributed to, those grim, lonely years. Neither the jocks, nor the heads, nor even the brains wanted any part of me. They talked *about* me, but they didn't talk *to* me, or even look at me, and if it weren't for the series of successively more hostile prank phone calls that I received, I could have happily deluded myself into thinking that none of them knew I existed.

Gym class, however, was where they allowed themselves to express their disdain. In gym class for some reason they were allowed to heap derision on the apraxic kids. ("No batter, no batter. Easy out.") Gym class was, of course, where the strongest, best-looking kids were made captains and chose us spazzes last. More important, it was where the figures of supposed authority allowed them to do so. Forget the work our parents did molding our minds and values.

Everything fell apart as soon as we put on those maroon polyester gym suits.

And dodgeball. God, dodgeball. As my own children were planning their tactics, evaluating which kids would be easily taken out by a hail of red balls (considerations included general athletic ability, low versus high center of gravity, established cowardice in the face of hard throws), I was rocketed back to those dreaded days on the blacktop at GW Junior High. I remember quaking under the gaze of a huge blond girl who even then I knew was destined to consider eighth grade as the apogee of her life. She smiles, heaves back her strong arm, and whales the ball. Before it even begins its arc through the air, I'm on the ground, quivering, arms over my head, already crying, even though I haven't been hit yet.

"I'm calling your gym teacher," I announced.

My children stared at me, mouths agape.

"What are you talking about?" Sophie said.

"You can't play dodgeball. It's cruel."

"It is not," wailed my son.

"Yes it is," I said. "It's mean! It's mean to pick on a kid because she's weak, because she can't catch a ball, or duck, or run fast enough."

The children looked at each other and then at me. Clearly, the more barbaric aspects of the game had not even penetrated their consciousness.

"Mom," my daughter said. "Please, Mom. Do not call our gym teacher. Please."

But it was too late. I was already marshaling my facts. The National Association for Sport & Physical Education had issued a position paper on dodgeball, and they didn't like it any more than I do. Dodgeball is not an appropriate activity for K–12 school physical education programs, said NASPE. A game that targets and eliminates weaker kids does not help them develop confidence. While it may allow for the practice of some physical skills, there are many other activities that do this better, without using human targets. Furthermore, the only children who like dodgeball are the ones who don't get hit, who don't get eliminated, who don't get whaled on. Like, for some reason, my children.

I prepared for my conversation with my children's gym teacher by learning by heart the following statement from NASPE: "It is not appropriate to teach our children that you win by hurting others." Then I made the call. At the time, my children went to a school where community service was an actual part of the curriculum. It made no sense for dodgeball to exist there. This was a school where conflict resolution was taken so seriously that when some neighborhood toughs threw eggs at the fourth graders, the head of the lower school brought them in for a mediated encounter session. This was a school that took very seriously the theories of Vivian Gussin Paley, author of the marvelous book on childhood social ostracism *You Can't Say You Can't Play*. I chose this school precisely because it was the polar opposite of GW Junior High. The gym teacher and the head of the lower school called me back, not a little confused, especially when I explained that while my children were enjoying themselves tremendously playing dodgeball, and that I didn't actually know of any kids who weren't, I still thought they should ban the game.

It was only while I was earnestly describing to the head of the lower school how detrimental dodgeball was to our children's developing bodies and minds, through the prism, I might add, of my experience huddling with my hands over my eleven-year-old head while dozens of balls rained down on me, that I realized that what I was really trying to do was exorcise the ghosts of my own unhappy childhood. I was stirring up trouble at my children's school because thirty years ago I was miserable, and I had decided dodge-ball was the very matrix of that misery, in which all the lines of force that were conspiring to crush my spirit were laid bare.

The thing is, my fantasies about being a parent always in-volved fighting for my unpopular child, doing for her what my own parents couldn't do for me when I was a girl. I am so ready to be that little girl's mother. I know just how to provide the proper sympathy, exactly what to say when the boys call out, "Hey, car-penter's dream!" (flat as a board, and easy to screw), or when she finds a Web site dedicated to humiliating her. My mother, as sup-portive and loving as she is, was always left somewhat befuddled and at a loss by my sufferings. "But I always had so many friends when I was a girl!" she used to say. Now that it's my turn to be the mom, maybe I overcompensate. I regale my children with the tale of how I used to eat my lunch huddled over a book in a corner of the school library because the other kids wouldn't let me sit at their lunch tables. I comfort them with stories about geeks and nerds who went on to conquer the world.

There's only one problem. My children are nothing like me, and they can never quite figure out why I'm laying it on so thick. They aren't living out my childhood; they're living their own. Whatever problems they might have, and they've got plenty, they're not the same ones I had. Sure, they feel sorry for me, or the me that I once was, but they don't really get it. Sophie is supremely confident, secure in her position in her class and with her friends. She's *always* been popular. She was the queen bee of Gymboree. Zeke doesn't have her social ease, but neither does he have quite my awkwardness.

And he loves dodgeball.

Halfway through the dodgeball wars, I dropped the ball. On purpose. Whatever I thought of the pedagogical value of the game, however confident I was, and still am, that it should be banned, my children are happy. They liked gym class. The other parents I talked to reported that their children were happy, too. Their children liked gym class. What my kids didn't like is their mother working out her adolescent traumas by berating their gym teacher.

There are times as a parent when you realize that your job is not to be the parent you always imagined you'd be, the parent you always wished you had. Your job is to be the parent your child needs, given the particulars of his or her own life and nature. It's hard to separate your remembered childhood and its emotional legacy from the childhoods that are being lived out in your house, by your children. If you're lucky, your kids will help you make that distinction. They'll look at you, stricken, and beg you not to harangue the coach, not to harass the mother of the boy who didn't invite them to the birthday party, not to intervene to rescind the lousy trade of Yu-Gi-Oh! cards they made. You want to protect them, but sometimes what you have to protect them from is the ongoing avalanche of your own childhood—crashing down on you like a hail of dodgeballs.

10. Sexy Witches and Cereal Boxes

There are two kinds of twelve-year-old girls: sexy witches and cereal boxes. Older teens still go trick-or-treating on Halloween, but they do so ironically, wearing casual, thrown-together costumes and affecting a jaded superiority to the hordes of smaller children for whom Halloween is Nirvana, the celestial circle closest to God. Twelve or thirteen is the last gasp of innocent devotion to the holiday. It's the last year that costumes are planned in the winter, refined in the spring, and constructed in the fall. It's the last year that a full-sized Twix bar will elicit rhapsody and too many vanilla Tootsie Rolls will make you cry.

In seventh grade, some of the girls will apply black eyeliner with a novice's shaky fingers, beg their mothers for false eyelashes, and slink around the neighborhood in their sexy witch (or sexy kitty, or sexy devil, or sexy vampire) costumes. The other kind of girl will construct bulky costumes that conceal as much of her body as possible, making liberal use of cardboard packing boxes with holes cut for her arms and legs. She'll go as a box of cereal, or a jack-in-the-box, or a box of movie popcorn.

When Sophie was in fourth grade, I was standing in the school yard watching the Halloween parade. The seventh grade trooped by, a column of sexy witches and cereal boxes. I turned to the woman standing next to me and said, "Which is yours?"

With a sigh she pointed to the sexy dead flight attendant: stiletto heels, tattered and burned uniform (with plunging neckline) spattered with Halloween blood. "At least she's not dressed like her older sister," the mother said, nodding in the direction of an eighth grader wearing hot pants, fishnet stockings, a bustier, and Vegas showgirl makeup and tottering along in five-inch heels.

"Wow," I said. With neither a cute set of ears, a tail, or devil's horns, it was hard to determine exactly what species of sexy the costume was going for. "What is she?"

The mother gave another one of those convulsive pick-your-battles sighs. "A ho."

"A ho?" I asked. "A ho?!"

"Yep," the mother said.

We looked back at the line of children, the lower grades now making their giddy way across the blacktop. "I wonder what kind of seventh grader I'm going to have?" I said. "A cereal box or a ho?"

"Which is your kid?" the mother asked.

I pointed out Sophie marching along with the rest of the fourth grade.

"Oh, honey," the mother said, sizing up my miniature flapper in her black fringed minidress, sequined headband, and rolled stockings. "You've got yourself a ho."

Sophie is fourteen years old now, and soon I expect her to issue an edict that I may no longer say her name in public, let alone publish it in a book. But while I am still allowed to describe her, let me state for the record that she is smart and thoughtful, funny and wise. She is just beginning to think about boys, and so far has concluded that most of them are either boring or gross. Last Halloween she appeared as Death from Neil

Gaiman's *Sandman*. She is no ho. But I'd be deluding myself if I called her a cereal box.

Sophie is not only smart—the kind of girl who chooses to spend her summer learning Japanese—but also tall and beautiful, with a head full of curls, lips more luscious than Angelina Jolie's, and a figure at once shapely and lean. Her legs are longer than her father's. Boys look at her as if they were starving and thirsty and she were a ripe pink peach.

In seventh grade I went trick-or-treating as a cancan dancer. I don't remember what I was in eighth grade, but there were high heels and leotards involved. And no cereal boxes. Within two years I had lost my virginity. I know for sure that Sophie is not ready for sex. She knows it, too, and has greeted my fumbling attempts to talk about the subject with horrified gagging noises and beet-red blushes. Sophie is, like I said and true to her name, wise, and I do not think she will make the same mistakes I did, but I worry. Oh, Lord, how I worry. And with good reason.

Throughout my girlhood, my mother regaled me with tales of the dozens of boys lining up to dance the Lindy Hop with her or to take her out for an egg cream or to pile their books in the library carrel closest to hers. The list of college boyfriends and lovers was long and diverse. African nobility and Quaker scientists. Boys from every side of the tracks. "Popular" is how she describes her teenage self. "Had a lot of boyfriends." But I can read between the lines. Girls in the late 1950s and early 1960s didn't have a lot of boyfriends; they "got around." They weren't "popular"; they were "easy." I know this is true, because the same was so in the 1980s, when I was earning my own reputation.

My undoing came in seventh grade, as the result of a sleepover party and a game of Truth or Dare? The question posed to me was simple. "When," I was asked, "are you going to lose your virginity?"

Today the proper pubescent answer might be sixteen or eighteen, or even, given the rise in popularity of campus clubs celebrating virginity, "when I get married." Back then, any idiot knew what she was supposed to say. We all planned to have a serious boyfriend in high school and—like the heroine of *Forever . . .* , the Judy Blume novel that was making the rounds of the junior-high-school set, its spine worn so that it flopped open to the sexy parts—present to him the gift of our hymen as a graduation present.

But I was a mama's girl, tied fast to the apron strings of a woman who had committed to memory entire chapters of *Our Bodies, Ourselves*. I understood that the personal was political, and that women's sexuality had been used for millennia as an agent of repression and oppression. I knew exactly why the Pill was so important, and why women like my mother were willing to lay down their lives for *Roe v. Wade*. Liberated women owned their own sexuality, my mother had taught me. Look at her! With her glamorous list of exotic boyfriends, she was ahead of her time.

"I don't know when I'm going to have sex," I said to the giggling girls lying in their sleeping bags in the basement rumpus room. "Whenever I feel ready. It could be when I'm fourteen, or when I'm twenty-four."

I didn't recognize my mistake until a few days later, when the prank phone calls started. It seemed one of the girls had spread the rumor that I wanted to have sex before my fourteenth birthday. She told two friends, and they told two friends, and so on and so on, until finally as many people were aware of my supposed sexual ambition as were using Fabergé shampoo. Making my solitary way through junior high school, I was both sophisticated and bitter enough to find a certain dark humor in the idea of having been branded the class slut when I had not yet done more than peck a boy on the lips during a game of spin the bottle.

It was perhaps because I had labored for so long under its undeserving cloud that when the opportunity at last presented itself, I eagerly matched my behavior to the sobriquet. In my sophomore year of high school, I was sent away to school in Israel. My parents hoped that a year on a kibbutz would inoculate me against the seductions of Jordache jeans, green eye shadow, and a too-literal adherence to the teachings of Bruce Springsteen. It worked; I was saved from becoming a New Jersey mall rat. However, on the kibbutz I was introduced to a whole different kind of danger: young men in uniform.

Ironically (to me, but not, I imagine, to those girls at the slumber party), I ended up having sex at precisely the age that had so horrified the students of George Washington Junior High. I was only fourteen when I slept with a twenty-two-year-old Israeli soldier. With the benefit of adult perspective, I would now classify him as a creepy and unpleasant sexual predator with a predilection for teenage girls. I was neither the first nor the last young girl of whom he made a conquest. Years later, when I was caught up in the Andrea Dworkin–Catharine MacKinnon brand of academic feminism, which vilified virtually all sexual contact between men and women, and certainly that between a fourteen-year-old virgin and a man eight years her senior, I started referring to what happened that night as date rape. When my infatuation with the antipornography crusaders ebbed, I stopped using that language and simply described it, if at all, as the night I lost my virginity to an asshole.

The truth, however, was that although I was not an eager participant in that night's activities, although it was scary and painful, and I regretted it even as it was happening, I did not say no. Nor did I say no to the other five or six soldiers with whom I slept that year. One of those young men could reasonably have been considered my boyfriend—we were together a couple of months—but the rest were one-night encounters from which one or the other of us ran, and about which I felt nothing but shame. And they were all far too old for me.

By the time I returned to New Jersey, I knew exactly what a slut was supposed to do and I'd gotten pretty adept at doing it. During my last two years of high school I had sex with boys in their cars, on top of piles of coats in darkened rooms at parties, in the back rows of the school theater. I snuck up to boys' bedrooms and smuggled them into mine. I cannot recall ever rejecting an advance, and I know I never felt good afterward. On the contrary, I felt used and dirty, at once manipulative and manipulated. I hated my reputation; I hated the sex.

I have tried, over the years, to figure out why I so readily adopted the mantle of school slut. At various times I've attributed it to a perverse need to fulfill the worst expectations of those around me, and at others to an irresistible hormonal imperative, the same one that inspired my sixth-grade Halloween costume—sexy Dorothy. It is very likely that it had much to do with simple insecurity. I desperately wanted to be liked, and although I knew there was no guarantee—and often no chance—of the boy's affection lasting beyond those few, groping minutes, I was so gratified by the attention that I could not refuse it.

But there is someone else I can blame. And really, who can resist fobbing responsibility for one's own faults off on another? At the risk of pissing off my long-suffering mother, I'm going to blame this one on her, too.* If I hadn't heard all those stories of whirl-wind teen romance, if my mother hadn't made a glamorous mythology of her sexual history, perhaps I wouldn't have ended up emulating it.†

College came to me, as to most kids, as a tremendous relief. Another month of high school might have found me out shop-ping for a black trench coat and an AK-47. But when I left home, I did not, as you might imagine, seize the opportunity to turn over a more chaste leaf. On the contrary, I had as much sex as ever—more perhaps. But at Wesleyan University there was no dishonor in being a slut. We were supposed to be free and easy, proud warriors in the sexual revolution. I slept with roommates and bandmates (although never at the same time), with frat boys and stoners, with exchange students and grad stu-dents.

By the time I was twenty years old, I was well into the double digits. Then I met Elan, my first serious boyfriend, and went into a six-year slump, in which for the most part I had sex only with him, and that infrequently enough. By the time we broke up, I was eager to dive back into the pool.

My dozen years of membership in the sorority of sluts ended on May 9, 1992, when I met Michael. It was a good run, productive

---

*My poor mother. At this point she has battered-mother-of-essayist syndrome. Over and over again I blame and abuse her, and over and over again, expressing nothing more than cheerful resignation, she buys dozens of copies of the offending volumes and gives them to all of her friends. Were she to finally snap and throttle me in my sleep, I doubt there's a jury in the land that would convict her.
†What a whiner. Really. Shouldn't there be a moratorium on blaming your mother for your faults after your thirtieth birthday? I'm going to declare one. As soon as I'm fin-ished writing this chapter.

enough so that when we engaged in the mutual confession of sexual history it caused the blood to drain from his face. The single digit I added a week after our first romantic dinner in SoHo is it for me (*kanehara*).

My sexual history before my husband is irrelevant, and my past as a slut is something that I mythologize, committing exactly the same offense I berated my mother for. And with two daughters, one of whom is approaching the age I was during the summer of my Israeli soldier, what am I *thinking*? Am I trying to guarantee that they follow in their mother's and grandmother's promiscuous footsteps? Am I dooming them to end up women like us, who lose count and are finally reduced to saying, "More than a football team, fewer than a marching band"?

Although I remember like it was yesterday two-year-old Sophie stuffed into a dinosaur costume, toddling from door to door on Halloween, my sexy witch is a teenager now. I watch her with her brand-new body like a too-fast car that she has not yet acquired the skills to drive. She revs her engines, sashaying across the room in an exaggerated approximation of J. Lo's groove. And the young men stare. There is something different about the older boys' gaze: they know how to drive that car. When I was fourteen, what I wanted in a boyfriend was just that confidence and swagger. I wanted someone who knew what he was doing, because I was just faking it. What I want for my daughter is the exact opposite. I want her boyfriend to be a pimply-faced boy her own age, blushing and gawking, with no more idea of what to make of a teenage girl than she has herself. I want this for my daughter not because I want to protect her virginity. I know someday she's going to have sex. Bumbling, incompetent sex, hopefully protected by lots of latex.

I want for her what I didn't have. I wish with all my heart now that I had had that first *Forever . . .* sexual experience, with a boy who loved me and whom I loved, after debating the pros and cons and planning carefully for the event itself. I wish I'd had candles and roses. I wish I'd had a condom. My first time lasted about eleven minutes, and I rushed from the room as soon as it was over. I don't even know how much blood I left on his sheets. With the perfect vision of hindsight I can see that it would have served me better to have fumbled through my first experiences with sex alongside someone just as unworldly. Perhaps then I could have kept the pace slower, not been tempted to try things before I was really ready for them. Perhaps then I would not have ended up living up to my reputation. One of the reasons we tell stories is to find meaning in events that seem devoid of it, to make sense of the senseless. Perhaps if my first time had meant something, I wouldn't feel like I had to talk about it at all.

It is possible, I suppose, that today's "hooking up" culture about which the mainstream media are so fond of agonizing has ended at least the social-stigma part of the teenage sexual equation. If I suppress my impulse to make light of my sexual experiences and use them as material for jokes, and instead tell my daughters how much I wish I'd waited, perhaps they'll just react with a kind of confused pity. People used to ostracize you for *having* sex?

But I doubt it. Things have changed so little. In my daughter's progressive middle school, a wonderful school in which a seventh-grade boy can happily announce that he's bisexual to no outrage or, frankly, surprise, they still use the same hateful language. Girls who do "too much" are sluts. The boys? There's no real word for them, or at least not one the boys are afraid of. "Dawg" and "playa" are plaudits, not epithets.

I have no social research to support this claim, but I see something hollow in all the boasting about teenage hookups. If in fact this boasting even occurs. How many times have we seen a wave

117

of adult hysteria in reaction to a supposed teenage fad that turns out to be nonsense? There were those high-school girls in Massachusetts who in the end *hadn't* made a pact to get pregnant and raise their children together. And then there were those "rainbow parties," which involved fellatio and different shades of lipstick and turned out not to be sweeping the country after all. I don't imagine today's teenage sluts feel much better about themselves than I did, back when I penned a missive at once frantic and miserable, begging my mother to come to Israel to help me because I was sure, after that first Israeli soldier, that I was pregnant.

I have no idea how to help my daughters traverse these rocky shoals. I have to trust in my guiding principle of motherhood: when in doubt, tell the truth. As seductive as it is to lie ("No, darling, I've never smoked pot," "I never spoke to my mother the way you speak to me," "I was a virgin when I married your dad"), it never works out the way you hope it will. Children are remarkably adept at sussing out the truth. Moreover, once you lose their trust, it's hard to regain it. And the price of losing that trust when it comes to sex in the age of AIDS, hepatitis C, and periodic mini-epidemics of syphilis is too high.

So I'm going to be honest with my girls while at the same time resisting the impulse either to make light of or to overdramatize my sexual experience. Because while I fear that making promiscuity sound beguiling and chic will lead them astray, I also know that the best way to ensure that your children dispense with your advice is to exaggerate the damage of the activity you want them to avoid.

It's like the D.A.R.E. program that was found by the surgeon general to correlate with drug *use*, rather than avoidance. If you tell children that all drugs will kill you (or all sex will get you pregnant and cause you to break out in pustulant, fatal sores), as soon as they are old enough to realize that their pothead cousin not only is not dead but has just graduated magna cum laude from Yale, they will dismiss *all* your warnings, just as the townsfolk dismissed the warnings of the boy who cried wolf. They won't listen to you about pot or pregnancy, and they'll also ignore what you have to say about heroin and methamphetamine, and having sex without a condom with a twenty-five-year-old you just met at a friend's sweet sixteen.

Moreover, I want my girls to feel *good* about sex. I don't want them to think there's something wrong with making love. The last thing I could handle would be to have Sophie show up one day wearing a gold promise-keepers ring and proclaiming her intention of "saving herself" for her husband. Don't forget that I was raised on a steady diet of Erica Jong and Marilyn French, and that I'm married to a man who turns me on as much now as he did sixteen years ago. In spite of my history, I love sex, and I want them to love it, too. The truth is that as unpleasant as it was to be called a slut in high school, and as hollow as most of those early encounters were, they didn't *damage* me. I long for different memories, but I am not a worse person for it all. I was hurt, but I am not harmed.

In talking about sex with my girls (and my boys, too), I want to invest it with the appropriate meaning. I want them to understand how important sex is, but also how *un*important it is. It's a part of life, a delightful part of being a grown-up. But having it or not having it shouldn't define you. And in the end, if they make a mistake, if they have regrets, they can always look for meaning in the way their mother has—by telling stories, by talking it through.

This is another one of those tightrope walks that make up so much of parenting. One misstep in either direction and you're bouncing in the net (or lying on the ground in a crumpled heap of broken bones, depending on how bad you've blown it). So far, thank God, while Sophie looks like a sexy witch, she thinks like a cereal box. Her approach to boys has yet to shift beyond the most tentative of curiosity. Unlike some of her friends, she's never "gone out" with any of the boys in her class, and she is only just willing to concede that there might be something appealing about that dude who played the lead in *Atonement*.

But I'm ready for her, and for her little sister. And for the boys, too. A while ago I ordered some condoms for Michael and me from Condomania, and when the box arrived, it included a gift: a pack of fifty candy-colored condoms. A Ziploc full of stick-less lollipops. I was about to throw them away (tightfisted as I am and as expensive as those fancy ultrathin Japanese condoms are, there's no way I'm letting anything Day-Glo near my lady parts) when I stopped. After a few moments of reflection—an internal debate that seemed at once to encompass every attitude, preconception, goal, and belief I have about parenting—I took the bag and put it on the very top shelf of the cupboard in the kids' bathroom, almost but not quite out of sight.

A few months later I heard a scream from the bathroom, as if someone had slipped on the tile and broken his neck. I ran in to find Zeke holding the bag of condoms, with his older sister standing next to him, her hands clamped over her mouth.

"Are these what I think they are?" Zeke demanded.

"That depends. Do you think they're condoms?"

"*What* are they doing in *our* bathroom?"

"They're here in case you need them, someday," I replied. "I don't want this stuff to be a big mystery to you. At some point *in the very distant future* you'll be having sex. And you'll need protection. Look," I lifted up the Ziploc. "I even opened the bag so no one will even notice if you take one." (I guess I should probably find out how long condoms last. Do they have expiration dates like cartons of milk?)

"*God*, Mom," Sophie said, turning her back and stalking out of the room and out of the cereal box world in which she will be living for such a very brief time to come, "that is so *gross*."

11. Rocketship

was four months pregnant with my third child, and we were heading to Hawaii on vacation. I stuffed our suitcases with swim diapers, sunscreen, and water wings, and bought a maternity bathing suit that managed to make me look at once pregnant and obese, a remarkable piece of structural engineering. I canceled the newspapers, put a vacation notice on my e-mail, and took the dog to the dog-sitter's house. I bought the kids enough new little toys to guarantee that I would have sufficient time on the plane to read an entire *People* magazine, if not the issue of *Harper's* I bought to camouflage my baser literary instincts. There was only one thing left to do.

The week before the trip I had an amniocentesis, the first time I'd undergone that procedure. My first two babies were born before I achieved the magical age at which the risks of amnio are outweighed by the chances of finding a genetic abnormality. I was only twenty-nine when I gave birth to Sophie, and despite the purple stamp in my obstetrical record that read "Elderly Primigravida"— the medical term for anyone who has a baby after the age at which it can be popped out during a bathroom break at the senior prom— I was far too young to worry about the quality of my eggs. Two years later, when I was pregnant with Zeke, I was still well within the safe zone. Even this time it was something of a toss-up—I celebrated my thirty-fifth birthday in my first trimester. I could easily have forgone the test, but I have always been a pessimist and catastrophizer. I try to claim as an excuse for doomsaying that anticipating the worst makes a positive outcome all the sweeter, but this isn't true. When things don't happen as I fear, I feel only a moment of relief before going on to wonder if there isn't another, more dreadful possibility lurking unseen in the shadows, ready to strike the moment I let my guard down.

Thus, when my obstetrician suggested the amnio, I immediately agreed. I remember the experience vividly, not because of the massive needle plunging deep into my belly—all the more painful because I clenched every single muscle in my body in order to keep from jumping at the sensation and causing the doctor to pierce the baby rather than the amniotic sac—but because of the image on the ultrasound screen. The first thing we saw were the baby's feet, two little pads with ten distinct pearl toes. Those tender, vulnerable baby feet brought us to tears. The doctor printed out a picture that would hang on our fridge for the next two weeks, and that now resides in a file, the most tragic of a pile of miserable documents.

"There," the doctor said a few moments later. "You see that? It's a boy!" Just what I—a fanatic devotee of the Oedipus complex—had been hoping for.

"Hey, little Rocketship!" I cooed. We had for the previous few weeks been calling the baby Rocketship, a place-holder name Zeke had come up with while we waited to find out the baby's gender.

When we came home from the OB's office, we showed the children little Rocketship's feet and told them that they would, in just a few months, have a new baby brother.

The afternoon before we left for Hawaii, I decided to call the

OB, to see if the results might be in early. "Just so that I have nothing on my mind while I'm floating in the ocean," I told her.

For a moment there was silence on the other end of the line. Then she said, "Are you sitting down?"

In my memory I am hovering by the ceiling watching the scene unfold beneath me. I see myself collapse onto the floor. I hear myself scream, my voice hoarse, my wails so loud it seems the windows might shatter. I watch my husband kneel down beside me and pry the telephone from my rigid clasp. I watch him cry.

And I think, "A person really does fall onto the ground screaming when she experiences a hideous, shocking pain. Remember that." This, alas, is part of what it means to be a writer, someone whose job it is to observe closely enough to convincingly turn what she sees and feels into words. A writer stands at a distance and watches her heart break.

We didn't go to Hawaii. Instead, we spent the next three days trying to decide what to do.

Rocketship suffered from a genetic defect known as a trisomy, a triple chromosome where there should have been only two. Down syndrome, on the twenty-first chromosome, is the most common of trisomies. Rocketship's was more rare, and at the time there was little research on the subject. We began almost immediately to scour the Web for information about the diagnosis, and by the time we showed up for our appointment at the genetic counselor's office, we knew more about it than she did. The one major study of the chromosomal defect evaluated the status of affected babies at birth, but not beyond. That study showed a good chance that Rocketship would be born without obvious defects, and a small chance that he would suffer growth retardation, hypotonia (extreme tension of the muscles), structural central nervous system abnormalities and seizures, facial malformations, failure to thrive, and developmental delay. There was no way, however, to know into which group he fell.

It was a roll of the dice, our genetic counselor told us. What you decide to do depends on how lucky you feel.

And there was the rub—one of the many agonies of this most tragic event of our hitherto over-fortunate lives. I, of course, never feel lucky. I had the test in the first place because I took the possibility of catastrophe seriously, even though my chances of having a baby with a genetic abnormality were, at thirty-five years old, only about 1 in 365. How could I risk another roll of the dice when I had already won the most miserable of lotteries, with chances far slimmer than Rocketship's? Months later, a friend would say that after you go through this kind of experience, your chances of having a healthy baby never again feel any better than fifty-fifty. You see the two pink lines of the pregnancy test, and you think, "Maybe I'll have a baby in nine months. But then again, maybe I won't. Maybe he'll be healthy. Or maybe he won't."

When I scrolled through documents on the Internet about Rocketship's abnormality, my eyes skipped past the reports of newborns with no apparent malformations and children of normal intelligence, to the ones describing predispositions to cancers of the kidneys and urinary tract or instances of psychomotor retardation. I looked up words like "dolichocephaly" (having a long, narrow head) and "kyphosis" (hunchback). I did calculations in my mind of what I could tolerate—physical malformations, fine. Who cares? I measure five feet—I bet there are parents in the world who'd be horrified at the prospect of having a child doomed never to grow taller than that. But developmental delay. That shook me to my core. Mental retardation. I couldn't go there.

Michael, on the other hand, always feels lucky. He is an eternal optimist. The glass is not merely half-full; it is a crystal goblet, a chalice of the gods, and its nectar, ambrosia. Were he ever to take the Internet happiness survey on which I scored a dismal 30 percent, he would score in the 99th percentile; I know this because I took the test for him, and while I know the results are only really an accurate reflection of what I think of his mental state, I am confident that I answered the questions as he would have. When Michael heard the statistical possibility of Rocketship being unharmed by his genetic condition, he breathed a sigh of relief. "We're safe," he said.

How could two people with such opposing reactions possibly reach an agreement on what to do?

Michael and I clung to Sophie and Zeke. I remember sitting on the couch, the two of them draped over our laps. I could feel Rocketship kicking inside me, his perfect little toes prodding the belly that had, until that moment, sheltered him so well. I concentrated on Zeke's silky skin beneath my fingers, on the smell of Sophie's hair, at once sweet and musty, like a puppy's. I pressed close to my husband and clutched my children and tried frantically to convince myself not to do what I knew, almost immediately, that I would.

For the next few days I continued my research. I found a therapist who specialized in people considering genetic termination, and for a long and anguished hour she tried to help us decide. We sought counsel, spiritual and emotional, from our rabbi. I talked to my friends, to my mother, to my mother-in-law. I e-mailed with a man whose son was born with the condition and was now a perfectly normal, bright, and cheerful child. One of my sisters-in-law knew someone in Israel who had received this diagnosis, and early one morning I talked to her. Her doctors had supported her deci-

sion to terminate. Their research indicated a higher chance of abnormality than did the single published study.

I found an Internet support group called A Heartbreaking
Choice, and the founders, whose heroic generosity I will never forget, in spite of everything that followed, gave me the Pyrrhic but
nonetheless tangible comfort of knowing that I was not the first
mother in the world to contemplate ending her baby's life.

Finally, at dawn on the third day, after another sleepless night,
I picked up the phone and dialed information in New York City,
hoping that the research scientists who authored that single major study would live in the city where their university's medical
school was located, and that they would be listed in the phone
book.

Miraculously, I found one of them. I caught her at her breakfast table. This impossibly kind woman did not hang up on the
stranger who disturbed her privacy. She seemed neither shocked
nor angry when I asked, in a voice strangled with suppressed tears,
what I should do. The doctor was kind, but she told me that she
had no information beyond what had been published. She had not
continued further in her research. She could not give me a medical key to unlock my terrible puzzle. But, she said, she could talk
to me as a parent. She told me that she had a son, a teenager now,
who was mentally retarded. "He's the light of my life," she said. "I
love him desperately."

I listened, wondering if I could ever be such a self-abnegating
mother. Such a *Good* Mother.

"But if I had to do it all over again," she continued, "I would
have an abortion."

I remember holding the telephone in my hand, my breath
caught in my throat. I remember the gray light of the kitchen, the

sun not yet risen. I remember the sound of her voice, and of my crying. I thanked her—for her generosity but, more important, for her brutal honesty. I knew what I wanted to do.

But as certain as I was that we should end the pregnancy, Michael was equally certain that we should not. For the next day we debated, never once with anger, but always holding each other's hands, weeping, apologizing. And in the end, my beloved optimist of a husband said to me, "I think, really, that we have no choice. If we do what you want, if we have the abortion, and it turns out that Rocketship would have been healthy after all, I can live with your mistake. I can love you, no matter what. But if we do what I want, if we have the baby, and it turns out he's not okay, it's too massive of an error. The ramifications are too lasting, not just for us, but for Sophie and Zeke. My mistake would burden them for the rest of their lives with the care of their brother, and burden us so much our relationship might be in danger."

I have never loved my husband so much as at that moment, when he sacrificed himself and his happiness to me. When he decided to love me even though I was not strong enough to give birth to Rocketship. When he decided to make a choice that was to him not merely incomprehensible but horrible. When he proved how capacious and forgiving is his love.

There was a single clinic that would perform the procedure, an hour's drive away. There was also a doctor in my obstetrician's practice who would consider doing it, but she was on vacation that week. And then there was a man, another hero of this least heroic of stories, a physician who had spent his career bringing babies into the world, and who had decided that what the world needed, what our community was sorely missing, was a doctor who would, with a sure hand, and a kind heart, ease them out. By the time we became his patients, he was exclusively performing abortions, one of those doctors whom pro-life advocates like to call mass murderers, and whose homes they stake out, whose windows they shatter with rocks and sometimes bullets.

Sitting in his office, I couldn't stop crying. Finally, he reached behind his desk and pulled a large stack of photographs off his shelf. The pictures were of babies. Babies of every color, shape, and size. For a moment, I wondered how he could be so cruel. Then he asked me, "Do you know what those are?"

I shook my head.

"Those are the babies born to women who were once my patients. Look at them."

I leafed through the stack. I wasn't the first to have cried over these pictures. Many of them were already marked with stains from other people's tears.

"Every one of those babies is healthy. Every one is wanted. Every one is loved," he said. "And you will have another baby. A healthy baby whom you will love."

"Do you promise?" I asked, as if he had the capacity to grant the wish. As if he were the one spinning the awful roulette wheel.

"Yes," he said. "I promise."

On our way out, he took Michael aside, put his hands on his shoulders, looked him in the eye, and said, "I will take care of her for you."

That night I didn't sleep. I lay in bed with my hands on my belly and felt the baby kick. I felt him wriggle inside me, rolling and flipping, like a little seal in the ocean of my body. I felt sad and guilty, but I was just so glad he was moving. It was the last I would feel of him. The last I would know him. Fully aware of the horrible irony, I tried to savor every one of his last hours.

The next morning we went to the hospital's outpatient surgical clinic. While they prepared me for surgery, Michael met our rabbi in the hospital's chapel. They prayed, I think, but mostly Michael cried. He'd been trying so hard not to let me see him cry, as if only my tears were permissible. As if mine meant more than his. As if he was not suffering as much as—or more than—I was.

They gave me general anesthesia, and before the lights in my brain dimmed, I asked the doctor to please, please make sure the baby would feel no pain, that Rocketship would be dead before it all began.

The medical procedure my obstetrician chose to do was not dilation and extraction, the one that pro-life activists have managed to convince the country to refer to as partial-birth abortion. It was a dilation and evacuation, but the actual physical process is no less horrifying, and if horror is the justification for the partial-birth-abortion ban, then the legality of the dilation and evacuation will inevitably be called into question someday.

When women of my mother's generation fought for the right to choose, they did not need to confront the ugly physical reality. But women of my generation, women who hang strips of grainy ultrasound photographs on our fridges, women who watch on three-dimensional monitors first flickering heartbeats at six weeks, then babies who suck their thumbs and wiggle their toes at four months, cannot deny it. When we choose to have an abortion, we must do so understanding the full ramifications of what we are doing. Anything less feels to me to be hypocritical, a selfish abnegation of reality and responsibility.

Since my experience with Rocketship, I have come to question most things about the abortion debate, except my commitment to the right to privacy and to choice. In the deepest throes of my pain, my mother, trying to comfort me, told me that it was nothing more than a fetus, not a baby, just a glorified bundle of cells. Cells, I said, with fingers and toes, a tiny but visible penis, arms and legs and elbows and knees, and a brain, damaged, perhaps, or simply unlucky. Even though the Supreme Court in *Roe v. Wade* specifically declined to rule on the question, the debates about abortion often degenerate into an argument about when life begins. Does it begin at conception, at birth, at viability? Before Rocketship, I never questioned the terms of this debate. But now I worry that if all this hinges on the question of when life begins, then our right to terminate our pregnancies will be lost.

Although I know that others feel differently, when I chose to have the abortion, I feel I chose to end my baby's life. A baby, not a fetus. A life, not a vague potentiality. As guilty and miserable as I felt, the only way I could survive was to confront my responsibility. Rocketship was my baby. And I killed him.

I know my opinions on the subject are harsh and unpopular. Many mothers who have gone through what I have shy away even from the term "abortion." As if merely having once wanted this baby so badly makes choosing to end its life something different.

In the weeks following my abortion, I spent hours of every day on the Web site A Heartbreaking Choice, reading other women's stories, seeking and giving support. What drove me away, finally, was the language of discourse on the Web site. Women there did not have abortions. They made heartbreaking choices. They had "AHCs." As in, "After my AHC it took six months to get pregnant again." Or "My religious Catholic mother hasn't spoken to me since my AHC." The word "abortion" was forbidden, as was the word "death," and the word "anger."

But I was so very angry. Angry at fate, angry at myself. I felt like that epitome of evil: a mother who has killed her child. Whatever maternal crimes I had committed before were nothing to this one, mere whitecaps to this tsunami. If ever I felt like I earned the title of this book, it was then. I was not just a Bad Mother; I was the worst of mothers.

I woke from the anesthesia absolutely certain that Rocketship's collection of triplicate chromosomes would have done him no harm. I was sure that if he had had a mother with more faith and courage, he would have been perfectly normal. This certainty was hardly a surprise; a pessimist is committed with all her heart to the notion that the worst will happen, and the worst that could happen at that moment was that I had killed my baby with no cause or justification.

These feelings were ugly—too ugly, it turns out, for the Internet. I frightened the other members of A Heartbreaking Choice with my shame and anger. I made them uncomfortable—especially the many pro-life women among them—by insisting that we accept the term "abortion" for what we had done. There is no denying, I wrote in my posts, that this is what we did. We cannot hide from the fact that when Congress or the courts restrict abortion, we are the women they are talking about. Our refusal to confront this truth will be the undoing of the women who come after us. If we allow the language of the debate to encompass only the experience of those women who abort for what others like to call "convenience," and they themselves know as necessity, then we risk losing this precious right altogether. How many of us, I asked, would want to have been forced to carry these babies to term?

In the end, I and a small group of like-minded, bitter women with black senses of humor and hyper-developed political consciousnesses went off to form our own support group. A group that we, in all our bitterness and black humor, called the Dead Baby Club. Our club grew larger and larger. Once something like this happens to you, you learn that among the happy community of Bugaboo strollers and preschool picnics is a secret society of loss, of miscarriage and stillbirth, genetic termination and SIDS, like a single black thread winding through a length of white silk. The club has more members than you would believe.

The Dead Baby Club met regularly. We worked our way through the restaurants of the Bay Area, weeping in one after the other, frightening waiters and driving away customers. We shared an embarrassing fury at pregnant women, whom we considered ridiculously naive. We used to joke that we would take our lunch one day to our obstetrician's office and tell our stories in the waiting room, just to teach the smug pregnant ladies a lesson. Yeah, maybe you'll have a baby. And maybe you won't.

This anger was a kind of insanity, one of Kübler-Ross's stages of grief, I suppose, that was alleviated in the end only by becoming pregnant again. One by one most of the women in the Dead Baby Club got pregnant. I did, after five long months, during which I sank into a despair unlike any I experienced before or since. Although none of us ever again approached pregnancy with the blissful hopefulness of an unburdened mother, we all managed to pass through and out of our fury. After a while we were able once again to express congratulations to other pregnant women, rather than issuing dire and dour warnings.

On Yom Kippur, the day when Jews gather and confess our sins to ourselves and each other and request absolution from our God, I wrote a letter to Rocketship and read it aloud in our synagogue. Because I don't believe in the kind of God that sits in judgment on our confessions, I did not atone before God. Rather, I atoned before my community, my family, and myself. I atoned before my husband, and my baby. I begged Rocketship's forgiveness for being so inadequate a mother that I could not accept an imperfect child. I told him that I wished I was more like his father. I wished I had been able to play the odds.

When the day of fasting was over, I did not feel an immediate sense of release. I did not forgive myself right away—nor have I yet, nor will I ever—but I did feel the beginning of an easing, a slight shifting in the way I was experiencing the guilt.

Before Rocketship, I had published the first few of my Mommy-Track mysteries, lighthearted little novels featuring a heroine who cracks jokes about being a mom while she solves the many murders that crop up in her peculiarly fatal corner of suburban Los Angeles. But in the immediate aftermath of the abortion, I found it impossible to return to those books. I had no funny in me about motherhood. I felt like the worst Bad Mother in the world, a mother who had killed her baby. What could possibly be funny about that?

Yet I also found myself desperate to write. I had the sense that I wasn't ever going to understand and learn to live with what had happened unless I wrote about it. I wasn't going to return to even a facsimile of the person I'd been before without the comfort of solitude and words.

I could not, at first, write directly about Rocketship. The pain was too fresh, and I lacked the necessary perspective and emotional distance. Instead, I wrote a novel, *Daughter's Keeper*, which I intended to be a manifesto, a screed against the destruction of society wrought by the War on Drugs. Instead, and inevitably, I suppose, I wrote a novel about a mother who loses her daughter. I wrote a novel about the debts a mother owes her children, even when the children are themselves adults. I wrote about the fear that your child will be taken away, or that you will drive her away, and the shame of making a decision that prioritizes your needs above hers. I gave the mother and daughter in the novel an ending that, although bittersweet, redeemed the mother's love. Feeling like the worst mother in the world, I gave the mother in my novel a chance to be good.

It was as though I were writing in concentric rings around the heart of what happened—*Daughter's Keeper* the farthest out. Some time passed, and I felt like I could jump one circle in, but only one. I wrote a short story about a mother who breast-feeds the ghost of her dead baby. The story is creepy and frightening and, like all ghost stories, turns a real pain into a supernatural one, thus making it easier to stomach. One ring closer to the truth of Rocketship was my novel *Love and Other Impossible Pursuits*, where I confronted full force the terrible grief and guilt of a mother whose baby has died.

And now, with this eleventh of eighteen chapters, I am in the innermost ring, the core of the circle. This is the first time I have written with such detail about what happened to Rocketship, about what I did and how I felt. And because I can write about Rocketship, I can accept that all wounds, even the most painful, finally heal.

Aborting my baby is the most serious of the many maternal crimes I tally in my head when I am at my lowest, when the Bad Mother label seems to fit best. But although I still sometimes find myself in that place of judgment, I also know that my children need me too much for me to waste my time on the malignant indulgence of guilt.

The morning of the first Mother's Day after the abortion Michael led me to the window of our bedroom and pointed out into the yard. In a patch of earth next to our front gate, he had planted a slender plum sapling.

"Happy Mother's Day," he said. "I love you."

Rocketship would have been eight years old this year. In those eight years the sapling has grown into a tree, its trunk four hand spans round, its masses of leaves golden red in the spring sun. "Rocketship's tree" we call it. This spring, for the first time, the tree bore fruit, little purple plums that we were at first afraid to eat. Sophie was the only one brave enough to pop a plum into her mouth. Her smile was wide. "Delicious!" she said. "Perfect!" She handed me a plum.

I bit into it. The ripe flesh was sweet, sweeter than any plum I'd ever eaten. But the inside of the skin was sour. Not inedible, but a little zing of tartness against my tongue, a reminder of both joy and pain.

12. A Nose for Bad News

One evening not long ago, while enjoying a family dinner at the kids' favorite restaurant, a diner owned by members of the band Green Day that specializes in meat loaf and milk shakes served by be-pierced young people suffering from a desperate surfeit of cool, Michael and I discovered that we have been under surveillance. The night before we had gotten into a fight—neither a rare nor a common occurrence. Michael and I see eye to eye on almost every question of importance that arises in our household, we enjoy no one's company as much as each other's, we spend the vast majority of each day together, but every so often things take a turn for the bombastic. Over the course of a marriage of a certain length—we've been married for fifteen years—all arguments tend to coalesce and devolve into a meta-argument, an argument about the nature of the argument, revolving around slippery questions such as who started the argument, who was the one doing the yelling, whether an apology is required, by whom any such apology should be offered first, whether the resulting tone of contrition is genuine or adequate, and so on. The fundamental absurdity of the process, and the fact that both of us care far more for each other than for it, means that while our fights are loud and all-consuming, they never last for more than a few minutes, and are usually resolved when I storm out of the house, drive around the block a few times, and return, bored or contrite. Never once in fifteen years of passion and debate have we gone to bed angry, and by the next day neither of us can recall much of what happened.

We live in an old house with, we thought, solid, thick walls. And thus we were stunned to find out that Sophie had heard our fight. Sitting amid the hipsters and alt-rock junkies with their barbed wire, Japanese demon mask, and nautical star tattoos, the blood draining from our faces, we listened as she calmly recounted the argument in all its specific detail. To us this particular argument, whatever its source or flash point, had within minutes merged into the undistinguished gray mass of all its predecessors. But Sophie, it turns out, has a far better memory for our discord than we do.

"That was a very nice apology, Mommy," she said to me, with a hint of condescension in her tone. "Although you might have made it earlier on, the first time Daddy asked you for it."

My tongue scraped against the dry roof of my mouth. I took a drink of water. Then I said, "Did you hear a lot of what Daddy and I were talking about?"

Talking. Yeah, that's one way to put it.

"Yes," my daughter said brightly, "I heard everything. I can always hear *everything* you guys do and say." Across the table Michael covered his mouth in wordless horror. "But I only *listen* when you're fighting," she continued. "Otherwise I don't really pay any attention."

I turned to her younger brother, busy with his fried chicken and biscuit.

"Can *you* hear everything, too?"

"No."

"Thank God."

"I only hear it when you're doing mm-mm-mm," he said, giving his eyebrows a lascivious waggle.

I don't know why I am surprised by any of this. My children are moderately more precocious than I was—it took me until junior high school to start invading my parents' privacy on a regular basis—but by the time I was thirteen, searching through my parents' drawers and listening to their conversations were two of my primary preoccupations. Why did I ever imagine that my own secrets would be any more sacrosanct or less interesting than theirs?

My parents both worked, and from the time I was in sixth grade and my younger brother in second, we came home to an empty house. There were strict rules about what we were supposed and forbidden to do. We were to do our homework and walk the dog. We were not to fight or eat candy. Most important, we were never, *never* to watch television. Not once did we consider following these edicts, but in the late 1970s television was not the wonderland it now is. In the late afternoon our favorite reruns came on—old episodes of *Happy Days* or *The Mary Tyler Moore Show*. Occasionally, if we had achieved a deep enough state of desperation that we were willing to risk being educated, we'd even watch *The Electric Company*. But, while I indulged a brief infatuation with the goings-on of Luke and Laura (was it rape or true love?), the early afternoon offered little more than a wasteland of game shows and local news. Usually, in the hours before a decent show would air, I amused myself with exploring my mother's underwear drawer, the shelf on the top of my father's closet, his bottom desk drawer, her top corner bookshelf. My preoccupation, of course, was sex, and I was looking for anything that smacked of even the remotest licentiousness. It was the 1970s, and my parents satisfied me with the occasional *Playboy* magazine, a dog-eared paperback copy of *Fanny Hill*, and the ever-popular *Joy of Sex*, that hairy-armpits staple of the fantasies of suburban teenagers across America. Once, during a disturbingly transgressive phase of all our lives, a copy of *The Joy of Lesbian Sex* even showed up on the bookcase, next to a volume of Victorian porn, *The Pearl*.

As I grew older, my interests expanded beyond the purely sexual. I rifled their filing cabinet, looking for letters and documents, preferably ones that would cast aspersions on my siblings or on my parents themselves. Panicked missives from deans of students, psychologists' reports, medical evaluations, accusatory letters from my father's ex-wife. I would tremble with a kind of delighted horror when I found them. There was no similar thrill to be found from the notification that my sister made the dean's list or a form letter indicating that my father's cholesterol was in the normal range. I took pleasure only in bad news. It was misery and only misery that satisfied me.

Neither were my parents' drawers the only ones that fell victim to my snooping. I was a popular babysitter, my services in high demand throughout the neighborhood. I enjoyed being with children and they liked me, I could be trusted to clean up the kitchen (when did that become an unimaginable request to make of a teenage sitter?), and, most important, I had never once turned down a job because I had a date. (Note to parents: Fun-loving social rejects make the most reliable babysitters.) As soon as my charges were asleep, however, I began rifling through their parents' bedrooms. I examined the vibrators in the nightstand drawers, opened the pale pink plastic diaphragm cases, stretched out on the king-size beds, and studied *Penthouse Forum*. In the last years of the Me Decade there seemed to be a fad for journal keeping among young mothers, and I read, my eyes usually glazed with boredom, endless handwritten passages about arguments with husbands and mothers, attempts, occasionally successful, at achieving orgasm, the trials and tribulations of potty training, and the machine politics of the PTA.

I was always careful to leave everything exactly as I'd found it, and while I could be wrong, I don't think anyone ever realized that their sweet, trustworthy babysitter was anything but. I should, thus, not have been surprised to realize that I'd gone and bred four spies of my own.

My daughter's admission that she pays attention only when we are fighting, given so casually, brought me immediately back to myself at her age, perched on the top step of the staircase, listening to my own parents' bitter exchanges. My childhood memories are restricted to the tone and volume of these arguments, their precise words and topics having long since faded from my memory. What I do remember is that listening to my parents fighting was not the terrifying experience you might imagine it to be. My parents were never physically abusive to each other; I could listen to them argue without fearing that they would cause bruises. At least not ones you could see. There was a certain thrill involved in eavesdropping on them, a kind of vicarious excitement to the drama of their discord.

That scene, the child at the top of the stairs, the parents fighting below, is a staple of the young-adult novel. As a child, I read countless renditions of it. But I never reacted like the characters in those books. I didn't sit, my heart in my mouth. I didn't weep soundless tears or clutch my teddy bear to my chest. I remember leaning forward, listening closely, with a kind of clinical detachment. All but taking notes.

I think my daughter is cut from the same cloth as her mother.

Decades apart, we both determined that the best way to figure out the complicated and incomprehensible world of adult relationships is to evaluate them at their worst, to dissect them when they are fragile, even broken.

She and her siblings do this all the time. Their father and I talk constantly—our marriage is really one long conversation, interrupted only when absolutely necessary. The children by and large ignore us, entirely wrapped up in their own complicated universes and in one another. They pay only sporadic attention to our discussions about our work, the books we are reading, the movie we saw the night before, their uncle's new job, the latest episode of *Entourage*. When we kiss or hug, their eyes skate over us; at best they snort in derision or utter a disdainful "Gross."

But let one of us mention an instant of conflict, let one of us recount a bit of bad news, and they snap to attention.

"What did you say?" Zeke shouts from the back of the minivan.

"Nothing! I didn't say anything," I say. My tone, in telling Michael of our friend's diagnosis of breast cancer, had not changed from the tone in which I described another friend's good review in the *New York Times*, but somehow the boy was no longer interested in playing with his Z cards.

"Yes you did. Who has cancer? Is she going to die?"

Or, "Who's getting divorced? Why are they getting divorced?"

Or, "Are you fighting? What did you say to Daddy?"

They can be so immersed in *Wallace & Gromit* that they wouldn't hear a bullhorn calling them to wash their hands for dinner, but if their father and I begin an argument or share a whispered piece of malignant gossip, they are like dogs responding to the sound of the can opener. They appear in the kitchen, their prying eyes narrowed. "What's going on?" they want to know.

*   *   *

Our bedroom door has a lock, and most nights we remember to use it. We've cleared out the nightstand, bought a box with a key for the things we don't want them to see (or show their friends). I've never been a fan of John Cleland, and *The Joy of Sex* is passé. There are plenty of salacious books on our shelves, but I figure once the kids can make it through the rest of a novel by Nicholson Baker or Bret Easton Ellis, they're entitled to enjoy the sexy parts.

I can handle all that.

The other is far more complicated. Better parents than we might manage rage in whispers, but to me the very nature of an argument lies in the fact that it is uncontrollable. An argument that can be muffled or silenced can just as easily be avoided. Anyway, given the keen ears of my daughter and the apparent paucity of insulation in the walls of our house, controlling the volume probably wouldn't make much of a difference. If I were a better mother, or a different kind of person, I might determine never to argue with Michael again. But the chances of that vow actually being realized are about as good as the chances of Dick Cheney or Sarah Palin being elected mayor of Berkeley. As a perhaps paltry substitute, Michael and I make sure that if the children hear us fight, they also hear us make up. They witness not just the bitter words but the contrite ones. In their turn they'll probably fight with their spouses, but they'll also be adept at the heartfelt apology.

None of us have any choice but to live with the way in which our children are making sense of the adult world, no matter how uncomfortable it makes us. What goes around, after all, always ends up coming around. Karma, baby. It surely would have made my own parents uncomfortable had they known about my childhood snooping through their drawers and closets, my listening in. But back in those days we didn't talk about such things. I kept my own counsel, drew my own conclusions. I never would have dared to cheerfully confess my eavesdropping over fried chicken and biscuit. Perhaps that is something to be grateful for. Because my own children feel no self-consciousness about their nosiness, at least I am warned.

My kids have put me on notice. They have advised me of their intention, like mine before them, like that of all children, to latch onto tales and examples of conflict, despair, misery, and sadness in order to learn what it is like to be a grown-up. This is what it has always meant to be a child. Such dark stuff is the very currency of children's literature and fairy tales. The stories my children love are full of doom and disaster. It's just like when they ignore our calm and pleasant conversation, but tune us in when we bicker. When we read, for example, the Norse myths, they stifle a yawn at the sun dawning over the green and lovely new earth, but sit up, eyes bright and fascinated, at the parts about Nidhogg, the dragon of destruction, or the hag with many heads. What is more delightfully grim and terrifying, after all, than the Grimms' version of "Cinderella," the one my children like best, complete with hacked-off toes and birds pecking out the stepsisters' eyes? I could try to present a Walt Disney version of my marriage, all happily-ever-afters, but they would neither be interested in it nor believe it.

So now that I know that they are listening at our door and rifling through our drawers, hoping we won't clean up our act, what will we do? Nothing different, I suppose. We'll just continue the show.

13. To Each His Own Mother

When my oldest daughter was in preschool, there was a mom none of us had ever met. The mystery mom's nanny brought the little girl to school every morning and picked her up every afternoon. The nanny came to Friday circle time and showed up for performances and events. We talked about this bogeymama all the time. What kind of a mother was too busy for the simple task of drop-off? Why bother to have children, we whispered to one another, if you had no intention of participating in their lives? Child neglect, that's what it was. A Bad Mother.

Flash forward ten years. Abraham is in preschool. His babysitter drops him off. Michael and I pick him up every day, but unlike the majority of children, Abraham is a Teddy Bear, which in sweetly cloying preschool parlance means that he stays in after-care until 3:30 instead of getting picked up at 1:00. He is also in before-care, which means he gets dropped off at 8:30. Because most of the children come to school at 9:00 and leave at 1:00, there are some children and many mothers whom I don't recognize when the day of his preschool graduation ceremony arrives, even though our kids have been going to school together for three years.

It's the final Friday circle time, and I am glancing surreptitiously at my watch as we sing round seventeen of "There's a

Dinosaur Knocking at My Door," when a mom leans over to me and whispers, "Wow! You're here. We *never* see you."

She has no idea how close she came to getting her clock cleaned. If I could only remember the name of that other bogey-mama of so many years ago, I'd write her a note of apology.

This was hardly the first time I was confronted with the tyranny of preschool expectations. Not long before the circle-time incident, the preschool class's room parent decided to delete the husbands from the class e-mail list, figuring that only the moms needed to be informed about classroom outings and schedule changes. We share those jobs in my family, and I sent back an e-mail to the group asking that in the interest of egalitarian parenting, the men be reinstated. "After all," I wrote, "if I have to deal with things like volunteering to serve pizza, then so should my husband."

In reply the group received an e-mail from a mom informing us that she (unlike, presumably, me) *loved* her children, and considered working Pizza Day a privilege, not a chore. I didn't know the mom whose ire I had sparked; I was never there at drop-off to meet her.

I forwarded this exchange to a friend, along with the expletive-tinged response that I would have sent to that sanctimonious mommy had I not been such a circumspect person. Except I didn't hit the "forward" button. I hit "reply to all."

Thus I guaranteed my continued status as the class bogey-mama. Clearly, the one who should have been banned from preschool e-mailing was not Michael but me.

Way back when Sophie was in preschool, it was so easy for me to pass judgment. I was a stay-at-home mother then. I relished drop-off because it got me out of the house every morning. The other preschool moms constituted the bulk of my social life, most of which had to happen with our children in tow. I had plenty of time for playdates, plenty of time to volunteer to distribute Wednesday bagel lunch, plenty of time to drive on field trips. I had nothing *but* time—long days filled with breast-feeding and grocery shopping, Mommy and Me and Music Together, playdates and preschool politics. I was certainly busy, but as my children were the source of my activity, it went without saying that I was there, ready, willing, and available for all the multitude of activities their lives required of me.

By the time my fourth was born, I was a writer working on deadline, trying to cram a full day's work into the hours before my kids got home from school. I took on more assignments than were remotely reasonable, but in all honesty it wasn't only my work that obliged me to buy out my preschool volunteer hours instead of spending time cutting up fruit for morning snack or taking home and laundering the costumes from the dress-up corner. The problem was that my fourth child's first year of preschool was my eighth. I'd faithfully attended eight information nights, fourteen preschool parent-teacher conferences, twenty parent-principal coffee hours, and approximately 280 Shabbat sing-alongs. Abraham was just getting started, but I was ready to graduate.

Abraham and Sophie had two entirely different mothers. Sophie's was young and eager, and found the whole preschool experience to be novel and exciting. Abraham's mother was old, her knees hurt when she sat cross-legged on the floor, and her cupboards were already bursting with popsicle-stick-and-glitter-glue picture frames. She did only a halfway decent job of feigning excitement at yet one more.

We have a *Baby Blues* comic strip taped to our fridge that offers an embarrassingly accurate reflection of our family life.* The first panel is captioned "First Baby's Pictures," and it shows a pile of scrapbooks and photo albums, painstakingly labeled and organized. The second panel is captioned "Second Baby's Pictures," and it shows a shoe box stuffed willy-nilly with photographs. The third panel is captioned "And So On," and it shows the parents looking at a picture on their cell phone and saying, "We really should download these one of these days."

I produced six complete, beautifully organized photo albums of Sophie's first year, the kind with the individual photo corners and the tissue-paper dividers. Stored on my computer are hundreds of files of digital images of her every smile, step, and bowel movement. Hanging on our walls are not one but two series of framed black and whites taken by professional photographers whose services cost more than my first car. I have a plastic storage bin full of videotapes with hour upon hour of Sophie playing with her toes or spinning the beads on her ExerSaucer or sleeping. We videotaped her *sleeping*, because, my God, no baby has ever looked so beautiful when she slept.

There are exactly twelve decent photographs of Abe's first year (and a bunch of digital images I will someday get around to downloading). The twelve photographs were taken only because we started this thing when Sophie was a baby of taking a picture every month with a sign that said, "1 month," "2 months," and so on and

---

*Can I take a minute here to complain about the un-magnetic fridges? My fridge was cheap; it is not a twelve-million-dollar Sub-Zero, although I agree those are very lovely. It *looks* like it is in fact made of metal. On our first day in the house I stood in front of it with our lovingly-acquired collection of fridge magnets and watched as they fell to the floor. Would it have killed the fridge people to make the thing magnetic? Is this some kind of implied condemnation of the accumulation of crap on our fridges? Where do they think we are going to put the snapshots of other people's children, the baby's first drawing, the take-out Chinese menu, and the dry-cleaning receipt? Do they not understand that their sacrosanct fridge door is going to get covered with scraps of adhesive left over from hundreds of bits of tape?

then at the end of the year framing all twelve of them together and hanging the poster-sized picture on the wall. We did it joyfully with Sophie, absentmindedly with Zeke, grudgingly with Rosie, and finally with Abe, only because not doing it would have given him too much to talk about in therapy.

We have about ninety seconds, total, of video taken of Abraham in the four years before Sophie's bat mitzvah, when the friend who was videotaping the event managed to catch him dancing with his sister. It was about time, because I was starting to freak out that if (God forbid) he was snatched by some crazy maniac, we wouldn't have a video clip to play on the news or on those huge AMBER Alert screens set up on the sides of highways.

It's not just that we are more distracted now, or stretched thinner, than we were back when Sophie was a baby, although of course that's true, too. It's that in some tangible way, we are different parents. Sophie's mother was twenty-nine years old; she was excited by every aspect of having a new baby. She was also tremendously insecure, terrified that she would make a mistake, and so intent on doing everything differently from her own mother that she experienced motherhood as a semi-constant state of second-guessing and reevaluation.

Sophie's mother hadn't yet learned that babies of six weeks have, basically, the same personality they'll have when they are sixty years old, and there is not a whole lot you can do to change that. You can do as much baby whispering and charted behavior reinforcement as you want, but the truth is that it's not going to have a whole lot of effect, either for good or for ill. You can probably train your baby to sleep through the night, but if your kid is by nature an insomniac, then the two of you are just screwed. You can probably make your kid work hard to earn enough stars on his chart to buy a Lego Imperial Star Destroyer, but if he's got a lazy streak, you're not going to have much luck stickering it out of him. And by the same token, as bad as your temper is, as prone as you are to nagging, if your daughter is by nature unflappable and confident, then there is, thank God (and thank Sophie), a limit to how much damage you can do to her.

Sophie's mother hadn't learned those lessons. On the other hand, Abe's mother was in some ways so laid-back that she once forgot him in an ice cream parlor. It was only a couple of weeks after I gave birth, and on our way out of the ice cream store I did that maternal inventory thing—kid 1, check, kid 2, check, where's kid 3? Over there, check. Dog, check. Sunglasses, check. Purse, check. Okay, let's go. I was halfway down the block before the soda jerk caught up with me. "Hey, lady," he called, trundling the stroller in front of him as he ran. "I think you forgot something."

Abe's mother got an early dose of perspective. When your baby nearly starves to death, when getting every mouthful of food into his body is a struggle, when you wonder if you will have no choice but to put him through a draconian surgery to wrench forward his sweet little jaw, when he gains a total of three-quarters of a pound in his entire fourth year, whether or not you show up for circle time becomes a lot less important.

Even the two middle kids had (and have) different mothers. Zeke's mother was, at least at first, pretty thoroughly depressed, and preferred to keep him reliant on her in a way his older sister never was. Each of the three other kids had Lovies—little stuffed animal heads with blankets instead of bodies. Sophie's Mr. Bun still lives on her bed, tattered and battered into nothing more than a bare, earless rabbit head with no blanket and only one eye. Rosie and Abe's mother was smarter and invested in half a dozen replicas of each of their "transitional objects," although it is true that there is only one truly beloved Pink Bun or Mr. Pup. For his transitional object, Zeke had his mother, or rather her boobs, which he relied on for comfort until he was two years and nine months old, when he began to make regular comments like "This titty empty. Other side, please." Sophie's mother was insecure and yelled all the time, but when he was little, Zeke's rarely got angry and, when the situation demanded it, usually had to fake even sternness.

Rosie, born after Rocketship, got a mother incapable of anything but the most shocking indulgence, who gave her everything she wanted, spoiling her rotten, and protected her from any and all sensations of displeasure and disappointment, no matter how educational they might have been. It is possible that the reason Rosie didn't walk until she was eighteen months old was that her tiny feet could not bear the weight of her rolls upon rolls of delicious chub (you have never seen such a fat baby), but it is also possible that it was because her mother, so grateful to have her, couldn't bear to put her down.

Abie's mother was at once much more strict and distracted, by her worry for his health, by having to pump breast milk, by her deadlines, by the sheer technical effort involved in getting four children from point A to point B.

It is hard to say which of the four got a better deal. Abie never had the pleasure of holding his mommy's hand during the field trip to the children's museum, and he was only ever allowed to have playdates with the two boys whose sisters had been in school with Rosie and whose mothers his own had thus made friends with when she still had the energy and spare time to do so. But his mother wasn't afraid so much of the time, or at least not of such silly things. He is also indulged and appreciated, even savored, because he's the baby. For all that he suffers from being a fourth child—his mother's preschool passivity, the paucity of photographs of him as compared with his oldest sister—he gains something from being part of a large family. It's easy to see what the benefits are while watching the four of them gleefully construct a fort out of living room pillows and cardboard boxes.

The little boy formerly known as "the baby" started kindergarten this fall. We have both, Abraham and I, graduated from preschool. No more Shabbat sing-alongs. No more preschool picnics or teacher appreciation breakfasts. It has only been a couple of months since we cleaned out his cubby for the last time, but already I'm waxing nostalgic. Remember Water Day? Remember that weekend when the class mouse decided, without notice, to go live on a farm in the country? Remember Friday afternoons in the park with the other kids in the class when I tried to pretend I knew everyone's names, but confused Parker with that other kid—was it Adam?—with a regularity that I know was perceived as intentional. What *was* that boy's name? *Was* it Adam? Or was it Jonah? Wait, I think Jonah was a kid in Sophie's class.

Come September, I'll have a whole new group of parents not to get to know. Sophie's mother might have considered being a room parent, and while Abe's would rather have her eyes plucked from her head, she is making a New School Year's resolution. She is going to try not to be the mom that no one ever sees.

Unfortunately, all the kids except Sophie started a new school, which means three classes' worth of children and their parents, three classes' worth of picnics and potlucks, three classes' worth of field trips and garden tours. I know that even if I approach this with all the goodwill in the world, there will come a time when I hurt Parker's mother's feelings or fail to recognize Adam's father when we bump into each other at Peet's Coffee. Whatever my intentions, I am probably doomed to become once again that mother to whom people say, "You're here! What a surprise. We never see you."

But the kids are older now, and many of even the most die-hard stay-at-home mothers have gone back to work, at least part-time. When one of them comes up to Abe's mother and says, a note of hesitation in her voice, "You're Max's mom, right?" Abe's mother will just smile and then maybe suggest they go out for coffee. You can always find at least one kindred spirit, even in kindergarten.

14. Legacy

Rosie and Zeke have Michael's eyes. The shade ranges, depending on mood and weather, between the color of cobalt blue glass and a paler, sweeter robin's egg blue. Sophie and Abe have my eyes: sea green with splotches of hazel. The girls' eyes are deep set and a little close together, like those of everyone on Michael's mother's side of the family. Abe and Zeke have long, tangled eyelashes, just like my younger brother, lashes so long they brush uncomfortably against the lenses of their sunglasses. The girls' lashes are short, like mine, an injustice, according to Sophie, of near-monumental proportions. "What is the point of *them* getting Uncle Paul's lashes?" she says. "Nobody *cares* how long a boy's lashes are."

We know where the children's eyes come from, just like we know where Rosie gets her little shiksa nose—Michael's mother—and where Sophie gets her short waist and endless legs—also Michael's mother; those are some seriously dominant genes. Sophie and Abe have their father's lips, Rosie her grandmother's, and Zeke mine.

Each of our four children is a conglomeration of features and characteristics easily traced back to one of their immediate ancestors. The parts that seem to have sprung from nowhere, like Rosie's waist-length blond hair or the fur on Abe's back, are just legacies of relatives whom we have forgotten. Our genetic legacy is like a drawerful of Legos, hundreds of tiny pieces that can be snapped together in near-infinite numbers of ways. One of the delights of genetic parenthood is seeing the different unique and fabulous constructions that spring from that drawer of building blocks.

But there are pieces of our genetic legacies, ugly brown blocks in the jumble of blues, yellows, reds, and greens, that I watch for not with excitement but with dread. Bipolar disorder so dominates my father's side of the family that I fear there is little chance of all four of my children surviving unscathed. Of all my Bad Mother anxieties, this is the worst. The idea that lurking in my DNA is something that could hurt my children so profoundly is terrifying.

In the scheme of genetically linked illnesses, bipolar disorder cannot compete with the pros. Unlike Huntington's chorea or Marfan syndrome, it probably will not kill them. They won't spend their young adulthoods waiting for a lung transplant like sufferers of cystic fibrosis. But bipolar disorder can make you terribly unhappy, so miserable that the rate of suicide is fifteen to twenty-two times that of the normal population.

My family came to know bipolar disorder under its original name, manic depression, when one of my relatives succumbed in a manner that forced us out of our state of ignorance (or denial). One of the many miseries of bipolar disorder is that it causes you to do things that humiliate you and the people around you. It makes you ashamed of your behavior and of yourself.

Suddenly things made sense, the way the right combination causes the workings of a lock to snap, tumble, and click into place. We understood the source of my father's mercurial personality. While it was frightening to confront this truth, it was also a tremendous relief to give our experience a name.

For most of his life my father cycled through moods at a dizzying pace. Even those of us who know him best were never able to get used to it. When I was a kid, my father seemed to exist on a schedule of alternating days. One day he was energetic and lively, full of stories and opinions. He would make you a cup of tea for breakfast, drive you to school, and slip you a few bucks even if you hadn't asked for it.

When he was up, my father was magnetic. He's a small man, no more than five feet five even before age lopped a good two inches off his height. But although he might not have had the actual inches, he had the stature of a much taller person. No one looked down on him. He was funny and fascinating, the kind of man other men liked to listen to. And other women, too, it turned out.

But on his down days he was impossible. Wrapped in a cloak of impenetrable silence, he would sit at his end of the kitchen table, his head bent over his plate, slowly and methodically eating his dinner. Only an idiot would risk talking to him when he was in one of those moods. While his flashes of rage were rare, they were terrifying, much worse than my mother's more frequent fits of temper. But most of the time he didn't get angry. He just sat there beneath a dismal cloud of gloom that made its inexorable way over the rest of the table, so in the end we all felt nearly as miserable as he did.

Despair was a virus working its way through the house like a pernicious flu in the wintertime. Before the diagnosis we had no words to describe my father's moods, and because we didn't understand them to be endogenous, we accepted his judgment about the state of the world, and of our family. In a sense, we suffered from bipolar disorder along with him. When he was happy and optimistic, we were happy and optimistic, too. Things were going swimmingly; the world was a delightful place, and we were the happiest family in it. His job was great, my mom's job was great, my little brother and I were gifted students with rosy futures. When his mood plummeted, when he could barely rouse himself from his bed in the morning, we understood that we were fucked. All of us. We had no money, we'd never have any money, my brother and I would never live up to our potential, if we even had any potential. For years—no, for *decades*—we all cycled back and forth, unknowingly caught in the sway of his disease.

My father was put on lithium, a common treatment for bipolar disorder. There was an improvement, although hardly as dramatic as we all had hoped for. He seemed to cycle less—his lows were not quite as devastating, his highs nowhere near as much fun. Without those regular bouts of hypomania, he was much less productive and took to spending more and more of his time sitting on the couch immersed in a book of Soviet history or a biography of Abraham Lincoln and drinking glass after glass of that toxic concoction of Coca-Cola and orange juice that I sometimes wondered might not be in part to blame for his troubles. (Surely something so foul can't be regularly ingested without noxious repercussions.)

Psychiatric medication is not a panacea, although it can be critical to keeping most bipolar patients from spiraling into an unconquerable despair or, worse, flying into a mania that, if left unchecked, ends up with them handing $100,000 checks to bankroll the lawsuits of heirs to Nigerian fortunes and donning foil hats to keep the government from using microwaves to insert thoughts into their heads. The various SSRIs and mood stabilizers rarely work as well as they should, and every one has side effects that often seem worse than the ailments they are trying to treat. What's an aluminum hat when compared with morbid obesity, diabetes, and a loss of libido so complete that you can no longer remember your sexual orientation?

After my father's diagnosis, it became clear that at least some of his six children inherited the genetic aberration, the as-yet-un-mapped bit of DNA that causes the disease. Two of my siblings have struggled both with mania and depression and have conse-quently led disappointed lives on the periphery of society and even their family.

On this evidence alone I would be terrified that my children would also fall prey to the disease, but of course it is not the fact of my family's diagnoses that wakes me up in the night and sends me to stand over my children's beds, searching their smooth brows and sleep-flushed faces for signs of melancholy or euphoria.

I'm scared for them because I am bipolar, too.

Like my father and my siblings, I resisted diagnosis at first, denying the inevitable, until I realized that I was doing to my own children exactly what my father had done to me. I was terrified that, like me at their age, my children had become little mood rings on the fingers of my hand, constantly calibrating and recali-brating my shifting temper. When I was happy and calm—which was most of the time—they allowed themselves to relax: life was good, all was well with the world. But when I lost control, when I yelled at the poor clerk behind the counter at the dry cleaner's be-cause of a burn mark on a shirt collar, or shut myself in my room and cried at the hash I had made of my life and career, they inched closer to their father, looking to him for reassurance that things were not as dire as they feared.

My children are luckier than I was. Michael has a far sunnier disposition than my mother, he is by nature optimistic and cheer-ful, and the force of his goodwill has kept them from losing their faith in the world or in their mother. But there is no doubt that I can be scary, especially when I lose myself in what psychiatrists call a "mixed state," when one's mood is low but one's energy is high. In a mixed state, a red haze of anxiety and rage takes over my brain and makes me say and do unforgivable things, until my better nature shakes off the demon and promptly sinks into depression as I realize the damage I have wrought.

After a lifetime of struggling with my moods, of cycles of rage and euphoria, of bouts of optimistic productivity alternating with pessimistic despair, I finally went to see a psychiatrist when I realized that things had gotten to the point where they threatened the stability of my marriage and my family. I had to get treatment, for the sake of my kids and my husband.

I began taking a low dose of an SSRI, and I noticed the change right away. I no longer found myself exploding with unwarranted anger at Michael, at the kids, or at bank tellers. I did not wake in the morning and consider my life, my family, and my work with a morose and helpless gloom. On the contrary. I felt *light*. It was as though the acrid gray fog that had been poisoning my perception simply blew away and I could finally see and be myself.

Then, after two weeks of pleasant calm, I found myself sitting in my bathroom, pants around my ankles, staring in shock at a pregnancy test flashing two cheerful pink lines.

I stopped the drugs right away. I made the decision on my own, not so much consulting my psychiatrist as informing him. I'd never allowed myself to indulge in much of anything during my other pregnancies. I didn't drink coffee, I went off ahi and Gorgonzola, I avoided the products of both Napa and Humboldt counties. It never occurred to me to stay on the meds. I wasn't profoundly mentally ill; I wasn't about to leap off the Golden Gate Bridge. I was just mean and unpleasant, given to fits of weeping and flashes of inexplicable rage. And isn't that how pregnant women are supposed to feel?

Except that I'd had two weeks of something different. I had had two weeks of contentment, two weeks of being in control. For two weeks when Sophie and Zeke fought over whether to watch *Thomas the Tank Engine* or *The Simpsons*, when Michael forgot to pick up the dry cleaning, when baby Rosie wouldn't stop crying, when an editor passed on one of my essays, I responded with equanimity, with disappointment perhaps, but never with apoplectic gall or soul-crushing misery. I now knew what it was like to be a person whose happiness was governed by the conditions of her life, not by those of her brain chemistry. Even more important, my family now knew what the experience of stability was like. Did we really have to give it all up?

I turned to the Internet. The pregnancy Web sites gave forth with a chorus of reassurance. Care should be taken, of course, but if my well-being required it, I should go ahead and take my antidepressants. Define "required," I thought as I read. How bad did things have to be before I could safely put myself in that category? I read further and found a Danish study that showed no damage to infants from maternal use of SSRIs. An analysis of Swedish birth records confirmed this. I was especially comforted by this last report. The inventors of the Volvo, the very architects of safety consciousness, seemed to be telling me that even if I wasn't in danger of slitting my wrists without it, I could still take my medication. I didn't have to be suicidal; miserable and unpleasant did the trick. The Swedes gave me the green light.

This time, before I did anything, I called both my obstetrician and my psychiatrist. The research I had found reassured them, too, and they agreed that I could go back on the meds. I took Celexa for the rest of the pregnancy, and managed to weather events, among them the death of my best friend, that would otherwise have sent me rocketing into bouts of volatile despair.

Since then, however, there have been studies showing that taking SSRIs during pregnancy can cause a series of neonatal problems. Nonetheless, the CDC recently concluded that antidepressants are safe for women and their developing fetuses. And by and large, they are. The vast majority of the babies of women who use antidepressants while pregnant are perfectly normal. But some infants present with a variety of birth defects and symptoms of SSRI withdrawal.

Abe had none of the birth defects described in the studies. Nor did he experience convulsions, constant crying, or breathing difficulties. But he did have that malformed palate, those feeding problems; he never learned to nurse, despite six months of aggressive intervention. When I read about these studies, I felt a nauseating twist in my gut. It sickened me to think that the treatment I took for my disease might have damaged him. For a long time I assessed every one of his flaws and minor disfigurements with the cold eye of a clinician, appraising and evaluating for subtle hints of gestational damage. I wondered if his chin failed to drop forward at seven weeks' gestation when it should have because of the medication I took. I wondered if his failure to latch onto my breast was a sign of something deeper and more profound. I Googled the words "hirsute" and "birth defect." I cupped his sweet, long foot in my hands and worked his little ankle, trying to figure out if the limp he had when he first learned to walk could really be blamed on womb positioning, as the doctor said, or if, somehow, the drugs that made me feel so good could have caused my baby to hover uncomfortably in the very place in which he should have been most secure.

I feel for the pregnant women facing this decision. It's hard enough to be either pregnant or depressed, let alone both, without having to make sense of conflicting medical research and objectively evaluate the quality and seriousness of your own despair. Add to this the cacophony of condemnation from the Bad Mother police, damning you if you expose your baby to medication and if you don't, and the decision seems nearly overwhelming.

Had these various studies been published before I became pregnant with Abraham, I would have tried harder to do without my medication. I would have tried, knowing the toll it would have taken on my older children, my husband, and myself, in order to spare Abe any potential harm. I would have done this, whatever my doctors' considered sound advice, bracing myself for months of upheaval and unhappiness and strapping my family in for a very bumpy ride.

But I didn't know. Those studies weren't available to me. It is of course not my fault—you can only make the calculus based on the information that you have. And so, even as I fret over the chances of any of my children becoming bipolar, I am especially worried about what I may have done to Abe.

Since my diagnosis, my disease has been more or less controlled. Unfortunately, however, medication and cognitive behavior can only go so far in reining in the bipolar demon, especially if you resist, as I do, the more hard-core drugs. Although I always take my medication, and never miss a therapy appointment, there are times when, in spite of my diligence, I begin to cycle. The red haze descends and I find myself lying in bed, weeping with shame because I sent a hateful e-mail, fought with my husband, or screamed at one of my children at the top of my lungs.

Of my various concerns for my kids, I think I am marginally more worried about *my* disease hurting them, warping who they will become and how they will live in the world, than I am of what will happen to them if they are themselves bipolar. But that's sort of like trying to compare my fear of being attacked by a shark with my fear of being eaten by a mountain lion. It depends on where I am; in the ocean I am in a semi-constant state of shark panic and don't waste worry on land predators; when I am hiking alone in the hills above our house, where the paths are posted with mountain lion warning signs, I'm not particularly concerned about being mistaken for a seal. I frequently wake up in the middle of the night with terror clutching at my throat and belly, wishing my beloved children had a mother who deserved them, and just as often I lie awake parsing out their temper tantrums, looking for signs of an unusual loss of control.

When I am feeling stable, I understand that there are worse legacies. I tick off the myriad of genetically transmitted fatal diseases. All four of Michael's grandparents died of cancer, as did his aunt and his uncle. God forbid he passed on some as-yet-unmapped cancer-related genetic defect.

Moreover, the dirty little secret of bipolar disease is that it's not all bad. It is often strongly correlated with creativity. I'm not the only writer who does her best work while hypomanic. When I am feeling most like a literary fraud, like a lawyer who managed only by dint of a lucky marriage to publish ten books and dozens of essays, I take great comfort in knowing that although I might not share the talents of the writers whom I best love, I share their disease. If my kids are crazy like me, they'll also be crazy like Virginia Woolf, F. Scott Fitzgerald, Leo Tolstoy, William Faulkner, and Henry James.

The buzz of hypomania is one of the reasons that I, like my siblings, refuse to take lithium. Lithium and other mood-stabilizing drugs work on mood from above, flattening the highs that can be so dangerous. Lows, while debilitating, do not usually result in an involuntary stay in the hospital. It's the mania—the spending sprees and racing thoughts, the paranoid delusions and frantic rages—that get you locked up. But I have never been manic. At my worst, I suffer from those mixed states, which are unpleasant and destructive but not dangerous enough (so far) to bring out the heavy joy-sucking and creativity-destroying artillery. And at my best? At my best, I am glorious. When hypomanic, I am busy and confident, vivacious and funny. I bring a laser focus to my writing, like a kid who pops Adderall before the SATs. I produce reams of prose of far better quality than the tiny constipated bundles I normally squeeze out. I entertain crowded dinner parties with anecdotes, and cheerfully volunteer for tasks that others avoid. In fact, one of my biggest problems with my bipolar disorder is struggling while depressed with the commitments I make while hypomanic.

Every once in a while the hypomania goes a little too far before it abates. I have to take an extra Ambien to fall asleep, or I monopolize the conversations at those dinner parties, unable to keep myself from interrupting. Worse, I over-share. I can always spot the other bipolar at the party. She's the one regaling the room with the hysterical tale of her husband's virulent herpes outbreak. Hypomania, like its bizarro twin, the mixed state, involves a loss of control. Normally people maintain a decorum in their actions and conversations that is appropriate to the circumstance they are in. Hypomanics lose that judgment. While hypomanic, I am capable of writing three books in a single year, but I am also in danger of posting intimate details about my marriage on a blog. The bipolar inability to resist the impulse to reveal inappropriately intimate details of one's life is why there are so many bipolar memoirists. Writers who lie, who try to put themselves in the best possible light, who shy away from the ugliest parts of the truth, don't in the end teach us very much about anything other than their own narcissism. It's only when you do the bipolar dance on the razor's edge of brutal honesty, when you are willing to put yourself in danger, that you can move beyond self-absorption to some kind of universal honesty. And yet, at the same time, indulging one's bipolar compulsion for self-revelation can all too often end up as solipsism. It's a thin, thin line, one that I spend a lot of my time worrying about crossing, or regretting having crossed.

However, while lots of us enjoy our hypomania so much that we feel an ambivalence toward the idea of curing our disease, our families rarely take the same pleasure. While they can appreciate our high-spiritedness and the fruits of our over-productive labors, the downside is too costly. Our families are the ones who suffer at the hands of our rages, and they are brought almost as low as we are by our despairs.

However much I embrace my hypomania, however much I'd love for my children to be writers and artists, to enjoy the madness of creativity, I love them far too much to wish this burden on them, or on the people they love. And so I watch them. I calibrate their moods the way they calibrate mine. Is he more angry than he should be after that quarrel with his sister? Was her wildness in the playground just high-spiritedness or did it evince a troubling lack of control? Is that *normal* adolescent melancholy? Is that a *normal* tantrum? Is he okay? Is she okay? Have I passed this to them, along with my green eyes, my short stature, my intelligence, and the shape of my pinkie toe?

This unremitting vigilance is itself a cause of anxiety. Even parents who aren't crazy struggle with the balance between monitoring their children and allowing them independence, between keeping them safe and giving them space in which they can make their own mistakes. For Michael and me, our inherent natures—his optimism, my pessimism—influence our different approaches to the way we monitor our children. Convinced that things could turn out terribly wrong, I observe and evaluate like a safety inspector at a nuclear facility. My dear cheerful husband (most often correctly) dismisses my concerns.

What happened with Rocketship was such a devastating blow to us in part because that bad test result bore out my pessimistic vigilance. If it had been up to Michael, we probably wouldn't even have had the amnio. But, unwilling to trust fate or probability, I insisted. And look what happened: as blessed as we had always been, here now the universe had dealt us a shitty hand. Being right about this added fuel to my fatalistic fire. If we could be that unlucky once, then anything—everything—could happen.

Since then, my eye for the evil eye has been proved right on other occasions. For years I fretted and worried about Zeke's behavior in school. He was unhappy. He acted out. When his standardized test scores came back off the charts—at both ends—I pressed his teacher about whether he should be evaluated. Something was off. Again and again I questioned and was rebuffed, told to calm down, not to worry so much. Finally, sure that there was something going on that we were missing, I insisted, over Michael's objections, that we take Zeke to a neuropsychologist.

He has, it turns out, a series of fairly minor problems. He has ADHD, and processing-speed delay, and a really bad working memory. None of these rises to the point of disability, and all are eminently treatable, and had I just insisted on testing him earlier, we would have spared him what was a truly agonizing fourth-grade year. And again with his little sister; for a year I felt like a neurotic nut, asking over and over again if it was really okay that she wasn't reading, even though I knew that it sometimes took kids a long time, even though it had taken her sister until she was seven to comfortably read a book. But I pushed for evaluation, and it turns out Rosie has a decoding problem, and now that she's got a tutor to teach her how to work around it, she's making progress by leaps and bounds.

So the vigilance works, right? Oh, the glory of being able to say "I told you so," a mother's four favorite words. Except that, by constantly watching for defects and disability, you run the risk of pathologizing your perfectly healthy children. You risk focusing so hard on the possibility of the negative that you lose sight of the positive. You risk, in the words of my friendly neighborhood Berkeley scold, imposing "your negative view of the universe" on your kids.

Because I know that I am by nature such a catastrophizer, and because I am really afraid of bipolar disorder, I run a terrible risk of seeing every case of the blues, every burst of energy, as a symptom. I cannot let hypervigilance define my experience of motherhood, or of my children's experience of being mothered by me, so I must resist the temptation to see every mood of my children as a symptom of a disease. I have to be vigilant, in other words, about policing my vigilance.

When I was about three months pregnant with Abraham, Michael and I went to have a CVS, a genetic screening test that we chose because it can be done far earlier than an amnio. We'd had one with Rosie, and were prepared for the experience. What we were not prepared for was the look on the ultrasound technician's face as she measured the baby. She stepped out of the room and returned with the doctor, who very gravely told us that the chances were good that there was something seriously wrong. The fetus was measuring far too small for eleven weeks.

He sat back on his stool and gently pulled a sheet over my gel-covered belly. "Are you sure about the dates?" he asked. "Do you know when you had your last period?"

"Yes," I said flatly. I had marked it in my calendar. Moreover, our obstetrician had given us an ultrasound early in the pregnancy, and back then the fetus had measured right on target, six weeks.

"What do you think it is?" I asked. "What could cause this kind of growth retardation?"

The doctor shook his head. "It could be one of any number of things."

I prodded and pressed, and in the end he was no match for the cross-examination of a former criminal defense lawyer with a geneticist's encyclopedic knowledge of what can go wrong with a chromosome. I could tell he was sorry as soon as he told me which defect he suspected. He knew that I knew it was fatal, that the baby would last through the period of gestation only to die soon after he was born. He cautioned me that there was no way to know yet, and that trisomy 13 was just one possibility among many. In a week we would return, and he would again measure the fetus and sample the chorionic villi so that we would know for sure what was wrong.

That afternoon we told our parents that there seemed to be a problem, although we said nothing to the kids. We couldn't bear to put them through that again. We made an appointment with the same gentle doctor who had taken such good care of us the last time we needed his unfortunate services. And we cried. Of course we cried.

The next evening was Rosh Hashanah, the New Year, when Jews go to synagogue and listen to the blasts of the shofar, the ram's horn, as it trumpets in another year's worth of joy and misfortune. After the sound of the shofar had faded, the rabbi stepped up to give a sermon about fate, and hope, and trusting in ourselves and in God. He said that if we set ourselves the task of hope, we may find ourselves rewarded in ways we might not have expected. I am not a spiritual person. I was raised by my parents to be skeptical of God and of religion. My parents so loathe religion that my father once told me, somewhat oxymoronically, that he would sit shivah for me (act as if I had died) if I ever became an Orthodox Jew. My mother complained when we told her we were being married by a rabbi, "Can't you just find a nice judge?" I do yoga and meditate not because I think it will connect me to the supernatural but because I want to lose weight and calm my nerves. But sitting there in the sanctuary, listening to the rabbi's sermon, the strings of Michael's prayer shawl looped through my fingers, I felt as though a pure golden light was being poured into my body. I felt warm and blessed. I heard a voice whisper in my ear. It said that my baby was *fine*. He was healthy. There was nothing wrong with his genes. At that moment I knew as well as I knew my own name that I would give birth to this baby, hold him in my arms, hear his first words, hold his hand while he took his first steps, and dance (*kanehara*) at his wedding.

My face was wet with tears, but I was smiling. I leaned over and said to Michael, "He's fine. The baby is fine."

"Oh, darling," Michael said sadly. "I'm so sorry."

"No," I said. By now the rabbi had stopped speaking and the congregation was singing, an ancient melody that connected me to my husband, to my family, to thousands of years of Jews blessing each New Year with the words of this song. "No, Michael. The baby is fine. I promise you. There is nothing wrong."

Michael looked at me, at first with pity, and then with a dawning realization. He says that he thought, "If the world's most pessimistic person has a flash of optimism and faith, who am I to argue?" At that moment he made the conscious decision to have faith in my faith.

If I was not wrong, then the ultrasound was. I called the obstetrician and asked her if she had ever had problems with her ultrasound machine. "You know what," she said. "I think it's been known to measure on the large side." Then Michael went on the

Web and did research on fertility and air travel (we had been in Italy the month before). It turns out jet lag is correlated with delayed ovulation. The baby was fine, I was certain. He was just younger than we thought.

A week later we were cheerful as we stepped into the genetic testing center. When you are expecting bad news, they treat you very differently at places like that. You don't wait in the waiting room with all the joyfully expectant parents. You are ushered inside, kept away from people whom you might scare and who might make you sad. The nurses were shocked at our smiles.

"The baby's okay," I said to them.

They lowered their eyes.

"Don't even bother taking off your clothes," the ultrasound technician said to me, urgently. "Just jump up on this table and let me measure you."

In the intervening week of sorrow and sudden certainty of redemption, the baby had grown exactly as much as he should have. When I went for that first ultrasound, I thought I was six weeks along, but in fact, because of my jet lag, I had ovulated a week later than I normally would have done. So I was only *five* weeks pregnant. The skewed ultrasound machine had measured the baby as larger than he was, a mistake we hadn't noticed, because it conformed to our mistaken expectations. The genetic testing center's scan was the outlier, but it was correct.

A week later, the results of the CVS confirmed what I already knew. There was no genetic defect. The baby was fine.

We had known from the beginning that we would name him after my grandfather, but it is hard for me to believe that it was a coincidence that the rabbi whose sermon inspired my faith was named Abraham, too.

As you know by now, Abraham turned out to have problems.

He was a sickly baby. But none of his problems were genetic, none were serious, and after the first harrowing days, none were life threatening. When I am in the throes of my worst anxiety about my children, when I seem almost eager to find issues for concern, I try to remind myself that pessimism has its price, and optimism its reward. I tell myself to remember that golden light of hope, the pure, joyful certainty. That moment, and the faith I place in it, are my legacy to my children, too.

15. Darling, I Like You That Way

The readers of Salon.com were very worried about Zeke. They were worried that he had been "betrayed and humiliated," and they worried that in order to please his selfish mother, the poor boy will have to be gay. The source of their collective anxiety is an essay I wrote in 2005 about gay marriage in which I recounted my son's comment "I think I might be gay." Lest you dismiss the hue and cry as more homophobic red-state vitriol, let me assure you that only liberals and the odd libertarian read Salon. The only reason the state legislatures of Alabama and South Carolina don't ban the site altogether is that, aside from one or two New York English professors forced by the sad state of Ph.D. hiring to relocate to Tuscaloosa or Jackson, no one in the land of Dixie has ever bothered to log on.

No; the worry, the rage, the horror, came from my brethren on the left.

The essay was about Zeke's (seven years old at the time) attitude toward homosexuality. I begin with a story about his best friend, a fifty-nine-year-old lesbian with whom he shares "a passion for the San Francisco Giants, dark chocolate truffles and New York frankfurters . . . Other than his dad, Zeke would rather be with Laura than pretty much anybody else, including me." Zeke has always known about Laura's sexual orientation, and her loving relationship with her partner is one of the many reasons he was able to muse unself-consciously about his own sexual orientation.

In the essay, I wrote about the moment when I first introduced the subject of homophobia to my kids, ironically at a moment of joy for all of us who care about the civil rights of gay people. We had always referred to Laura's partner as her wife, because, as I wrote in the essay, "there seemed no other way to describe that relationship in terms the kids could understand, in a way that would align this romance with the other long-term commitments the children knew—our marriage, those of their grandparents—and distinguish it from more transient ones." When Gavin Newsom, the mayor of San Francisco, first began issuing marriage licenses back in 2005, we celebrated, but we also had to explain to the kids that this was the first time gay people were allowed to be legally married in the United States of America. That shocked Zeke. He believes that you're supposed to marry the person you love, whoever and whatever that person happens to be.

But what really freaked people out was that I wrote that not only does the prospect of my son being gay not bother me but I actually hope he might be. The reason I gave for wanting a gay son was lighthearted: "How many straight men maintain inappropriately intimate relationships with their mothers? How many *shop* with them?"

I was taken to task for my biases. One gay reader chided me: "Shopping? Inappropriate relationships with your mother? This is not the 1950s and this type of stereotyping is insulting and one of the reasons it's still hard to be gay in Bush's America." And: "As a gay man, I found these comments to be condescending, out of touch, and quite a bit insulting. Either support gay rights or don't; but please don't equate them with some deep desire on the part of gays and lesbians to trash sex-role stereotypes."

Good points, and ones with which I agree. That's why I described my stereotypes as "shopworn and musty clichés."

However, at the risk of incurring yet more wrath, I'm going to just go ahead and dive headfirst into the roiling lava pit of bias. While I know and love a few straight men, for every straight male friend I have, there are three or four or more gay men with whom I'd rather spend my time. By and large, the gay men I know are simply more fun. My gay friends dish with more relish and verve. They have a better design sense and are far more willing to discuss the proper placement of a piece of furniture than any straight men I know. For a long time, being part of the gay community mandated a familiarity with a certain kind of culture. You listened to opera, you went to the theater, you wore something fabulous to a Madonna concert. This may be a function of my generation—do nineteen-year-old gay men even know who Barbra Streisand or Maria Callas is?—but I have never met a straight man, other than Michael, who would comb the antiques shops of Venice with me, searching tirelessly for the perfect tasseled pillow. As far as my joke about close relationships with mothers, I'm terrified at the prospect of daughters-in-law. With good reason: I am one myself. I hope my sons are gay so that they will bring home lovely young men who will redecorate my kitchen (another stereotype!). Zeke, his boyfriend, and I would be a giggling and gossiping threesome, going shopping for Jimmy Choos and beaded Victorian lamps (and another stereotype!) before the boys head off to a circuit party. (Now, *that's* just real life.)

Enough of the stereotypes. I do know some gay men whose ears aren't pierced and who've never evinced much interest in the Divine Miss M. They wear conservative suits (Brooks Brothers and J. Press rather than Paul Smith and Zegna); they wouldn't know damask from terry cloth; they are soccer dads and computer executives who drag their partners to auto shows. But even these men have a little something extra, if only the sensitivity wrought by dealing with oppression and discrimination throughout their lives.

From the time I was a teenager, and probably before, I was drawn to men like that. You already know what a geeky, unpopular girl I was. I lived in a wealthy town, and my family didn't have much money, but a lot of my unpopularity may have had less to do with my parents' inability to buy me peach-colored Izod shirts and Fair Isle sweaters and more to do with my moods. I wasn't necessarily a happy kid; in retrospect, I probably showed some symptoms of the bipolar disorder with which I was ultimately diagnosed. Outsiders flock together, perhaps because no one else will have them, perhaps because they know each other's pain. For whatever reason, among the few friends I had were scrawny boys with uneasy smiles who spent most of their days scrambling after the books the cool boys dumped from their arms or running away from games of "smear the queer." Not all of those boys were gay, of course. Some just turned into sensitive men, like my husband.

Soon enough, I had a better reason to like those boys. With my fellow theater rats, I never had to worry about my slutty reputation. They wouldn't flirt with me, fuck me, and then tell their friends. It went without saying that I wouldn't end up splayed out in the backseat of a car. We could be affectionate, even physically, without the specter of sex and its humiliating ramifications.

Now that I'm an adult, these relationships continue. A number of years ago, Michael and I met a gay man who had written a memoir that both of us had read and admired tremendously. After a few hours of enchanting conversation over delicious food, we invited our new friend to join us on a trip to Italy. For two weeks. I cannot imagine a universe in which we'd have dinner with a straight guy and immediately invite him to share our vacation rental. Our friend was every bit the marvelous companion we knew he'd be (note prior reference to shopping for tasseled pillows).

I have a remarkably patient gay friend who once accompanied me on a research expedition to one of San Francisco's most notorious strip clubs (for a scene in one of my novels, I swear to God). I was shy about going alone, but I was also embarrassed at the prospect of looking up some woman's vagina in the company of a straight man—these women are so naked that if I'd had a Q-tip and a speculum, I could have given a dozen Pap smears. I wanted to see what the women did to the men in these kinds of places, but I didn't want to be distracted by my companion popping a massive boner. Unfortunately, it turns out that friction knows no sexual orientation. I had to cut my friend off after three lap dances.

My affinity for gay men is probably one of the reasons I fell so hard for my husband. Despite what some continue to insist, Michael is straight. Yes, he wrote a book that can be considered a gay coming-out novel, and yes, he's acknowledged that the story was in part inspired by experience, but he's straight. However, he also loves gay men, enjoys their company, and is a tiny bit of a sissy himself. For example, he was the one who decided to see *The Devil Wears Prada*, even though it was the opening weekend of *Superman Returns*. He loves to shop; most of my nicest clothes and all of my jewelry were gifts from him. He appreciates music and art, far more than I do.

I want my sons to be just like their father. They may be straight, but unusual, like he is, but if they're gay, there's a hell of a lot better chance they'll turn out that way.

My own prejudice was on full view when I wrote about the idea of my daughters being lesbians. "Would a lesbian daughter give me grief about shaving my legs? Would her girlfriend the Gestalt therapist bring bulgur salad to family potlucks?" What that stereotype and the others are about, obviously, is prejudice and insecurity. "The stereotypical gay woman makes me insecure, conscious of my failings as a feminist. I make less money than Michael; I rely on him for simple home repairs; I care too much about what I look like; I once got a Brazilian bikini wax."

But the critique of these admitted biases wasn't the real issue people, even gay people, had with the essay. Many of the folks who posted comments were aghast because they believed that I had exposed my son to ridicule. They were sure that being gay, or just musing about your sexuality, would necessarily make him the butt of other children's bullying. That is probably true in much of what someone described as "Bush Country." But my family lives in Berkeley. There are many gay families in my children's school. The school shows movies like *Daddy and Papa*, and the high schools all have Gay-Straight Alliances. Our friends are as often gay as straight. My children's world, thank God, is nearly devoid of homophobia. Sounds bucolic, doesn't it? It is, and it's one of the main reasons we live here when we could live so much less expensively somewhere else. Bullying may have been the sad experience of many gay men, but I think things are changing for kids nowadays.

When I was an undergraduate, I went to a concert given by a not particularly talented lesbian folksinger. I have a perfect recollection of her hoarse voice warbling off-key the song she wished her mother had sung to her when she first came out: "Honey, I'm glad that you're gay; darling, I like you that way." That's the response my sons and daughters will receive if ever they make a similar announcement.

At least two-thirds of high-school students support gay marriage, according to the Hamilton College national youth opinion poll. This generational shift in favor of gay rights has been consistent over the years, and it explains why the religious right is desperately trying to amend the Constitution: they only have so much time before our more open-minded children are old enough to vote.

Other people were upset by my essay because they thought that I had unfairly imposed expectations on my child that he might not be able to fulfill. I think they are guilty of hypocrisy on the grandest scale. Would you prefer that your son were straight? Do you joke about your son "marrying" the little daughter of your college roommate? You, too, are imposing an expectation on your child. My son's sexual orientation will develop on its own, no matter my hopes and idle fantasies.

How many twin studies have to be done before people understand that homosexuality is innate? It has nothing to do with choice or a mother's smothering nature. People are gay because of genetics or fetal hormonal exposure or some other random physical and chemical spin of the wheel. Every time we have a child, we spin that wheel. Sometimes our luck is bad, like Michael's and mine once was. Sometimes it's marvelous, and fate's game of roulette gives you a gorgeous and talented gay son or daughter. Bless mutation and complication and all that gives us such magnificent diversity.

16. Baby Lust

The young mother wanted to be in that bathroom even less than I did. She scuttled out, her whole body curved in a protective crouch around the tiny bundle hanging in a sling from her shoulders, her nose wrinkled against the malevolent stench of a poorly maintained public restroom. I was there with my two youngest children because there is an inverse correlation between the cleanliness of a bathroom and Rosie's need to move her bowels.

While Rosie was hovering over the grimy toilet seat and I was herding her younger brother around the stall, trying to keep him from touching anything (one of my grandmother's most important legacies is the idea that the only part of your body that should touch a public restroom is the soles of your shoes), I caught a last glimpse of the other mother rushing out the exit. She had that swollen, stunned look I remember so well from the first months after each of my children was born, when "exhaustion" seems far too benign a word to describe the extent of your fatigue, when it seems like every part of your body is leaking and sore, when you have trouble remembering why you wanted a baby to begin with. The only part of her baby that was visible outside of the cotton sling was a tuft of mouse-colored hair. I knew how soft that hair was, delicate filaments of spun sugar. I could remember the sensation of silken baby hair against my lips, of a small, warm skull resting in the palm of my hand, the pulse fluttering under my fingertips.

Rosie was not quite four years old at the time, and Abraham had just turned two. Watching the new mother stumble away on shaky legs, I realized with an absolute and sickening certainty that I wanted another baby.

"Mommy, wipe me," Rosie said.

"Me poop too," Abe announced, pointing to his diaper.

I have four children. Four is plenty. Four might be too many, if one is to accept the opinion of the people who pass me on the street and ask, horrified, "Are they *all* yours?" Personally, I think four is the perfect number of children for our particular family. Four is enough to create the frenzied cacophony that Michael and I find so joyful. Four is not too many to sit in rapt attention when it's time for the nightly chapter of *The Wizard of Oz* or *The Twenty-one Balloons*. Four is a gang that entertains and protects its members. Four fit comfortably in a minivan.

Four children is enough.

So why can't I stop thinking about another?

This may be nothing more than the most biological of urges. I recognize it; I've felt it before, and I've seen it in my friends, whether they're mothers of one child, of three, or of five. When I first realized that I was suffering from baby lust, Abraham was barely two. He was walking; he had begun to put together simple sentences. He had even used the potty a few times. Even though we called him (and call him still, though he is now five) the baby, he wasn't one anymore, and perhaps my body was simply doing what evolution dictates; perhaps my uterus was sending a hormonal message to my brain as I watched him get ready to toddle off to preschool. Okay, Mama, this one's browned, cool, and ready to slice. It's time to get another bun in the oven.

I am forty-three years old now, and Abie is starting kindergarten next fall. And part of me still wants another. I know many women who have happily had children well into their forties, but I started this process younger than many of my contemporaries. At twenty-nine years old, I was one of the first of my friends to have a baby. I remember touring the hospital in my eighth month, waddling through the labor and delivery suites in my red-and-white-striped Betsey Johnson minidress (the only time in my life I have ever worn horizontal stripes, because, well, why not?), staring at the other pregnant women on the tour. They looked so *old* to me, with their gray hair and their crow's-feet. Almost a decade later, when I was big with Abraham, I could see the same look of pity on the faces of young pregnant women who bumped bellies with me.

My skin isn't the only part of me that's old. I pulled my back out twice last week, once, honorably, while lifting weights, and once, ridiculously, while turning on my bedside lamp. Perhaps this whole debate is just a pathetic clutching at youth. After all, wrinkled or not, if I'm toting around a newborn, then I'm young, right? But whatever the state of my skin and my muscles, we all know that my eggs aren't what they once were. With four healthy children, I tell myself it would be irresponsible to give the dice another throw.

And yet.

And yet.

Never again to feel the sandbag weight of a baby slung over my shoulder? Never again to hold miniature, translucent starfish fingers in my hand? Never again to match my breath to a baby's shallow wheeze?

I am carrying on such arguments in my head. I tell myself that after four children my belly is already so stretched and flabby that I have to do origami to get my pants buttoned—a line I have used before and one recently *stolen* from me by Elisabeth Hasselbeck of *The View* (although she was talking about her breasts—gross).

One more pregnancy and I'll be doomed to elastic waists for the rest of my life. I remind myself of what it would be like to confront the decision of going off my meds. I remind myself that it was one thing to have children before my diagnosis, but now that I know I'm crazy, how could I subject a child to that? I remember the look on my good-natured obstetrician's face when she said, while checking how my last Cesarean incision was healing, "I'm glad I don't have to go back in *there* again." Ethel Kennedy reportedly had all eleven of her children via Cesarean section, but I can happily concede that record to her.

Other women in the park are having these same internal debates, I think. When a newborn shows up, there's a pause, a hiccup in the general hubbub. We all stare, misty-eyed. We coo; we ooh. And then someone's kid whacks someone else's on the head with a shovel, or a toddler gets stuck on the top of the slide and gives a wrenching shriek, and we all briskly shake off that gentle longing.

My work, too, should make me want to stay away from the baby fog, whatever its seductions. When the children were very young, I found it difficult to write. Each time I told myself it would be different, but with every child, for the first four months, I would accomplish nothing. Even after I could return to work, I worked on baby time, stopping to nurse, to bandage wounds both real and imaginary, losing days to their sleepless nights. I find myself relieved that that time is drawing to a close. They need me as much as ever, but the way they need me is different; it's as intense, but it's not diffused over every hour of the day. They are gone at school all day, and with a certain amount of discipline I can devote that time to my work. I realize that I don't want to go back to squeezing my writing into the cracks my children leave in the day and in my concentration.

The very fact that I can have this internal debate feels like a kind of gluttony. So many of my friends have struggled with infertility; so many of them fight ferociously for the chance to be a mother to even one baby. And here I want to gobble up so many more than my share. So, too, for now I have the luxury of economic security. I can afford to pay for preschool, for summer camp, for a sitter to watch the baby during the mornings while I work. There are so many people for whom the decision to have a child is determined not by the tugs of their wombs or hearts but by the exigencies of their wallets. We are lucky not to have gut-wrenching financial worries, but like most families we live on the income we earn, and our financial stability depends on our continuing to work.

The real reason not to have another child is because, when I think hard about it, when I get beyond the smell of a baby's head and the way it feels to take a bath with a newborn, I realize that I don't want to be there again, that *none* of the members of my family wants to be there again. As much as Michael sometimes misses having an infant in the house, he likes where we are right now. Mealtimes in our house are as raucous and boisterous as they always were, pitched at a volume that makes the children from small families who visit our house quiver with anxiety, but now it's not because we need to shout over a colicky baby's screams. It's because every evening each of the four children has news to report, a perfect score on a spelling test that must be announced with false modesty, an injury, either physical or emotional, to recount with excruciating detail. They talk over each other, vying for attention, bickering over who goes first, and at the same time solicitously pouring milk and helping mop up one another's spills. Divided evenly into two sets of two, the "bigs" and the "littles," they engage in elaborate and protracted fantasy games. Abraham long ago graduated to the role of prince's page or baby dragon, instead of being shunted off as a piece of furniture or tossed out of the room altogether. Finally, he has evolved from playing a prop to being an almost equal partner.

Even recognizing all this, I was still idly flirting with the idea of a fifth child until one night a couple of years ago when it became clear to me that my own limitations, and the needs of the children I already have, made it clear that four was enough.

At the time I thought we were managing to pay enough attention to each of the children, to know who was anxious about the wavering loyalty of a supposed best friend, whose soccer cleats were too tight. Then the tooth fairy forgot to come.

It was Sophie's thirteenth tooth, and by now she had the system down cold. I wondered if she still believed in glitter-clad fairies flitting from house to house gathering enameled bricks for their fairy castles, but she wasn't giving anything away. She presented the yellowed molar proudly, and tucked it carefully under her pillow in the same little box she'd used for the other twelve.

The evening proceeded in its usual hysterical pace, an assembly line of bathing, teeth brushing, story time, and then each child demanding his or her very specific bedtime routine. One child must have someone lie next to her and sing the same two Pete Seeger songs, another requires an elaborate ritual of train songs in a slowly darkening bedroom. It is a good ninety minutes of tamped-down frenzy between the end of supper and lights-out, and I often collapse in my own bed not long after the kids are tucked into theirs.

Sophie's face, at six the next morning, when she stood over our bed, was one of barely controlled fury.

"The *tooth fairy* didn't show up," she said. I knew by the ironic and disgusted quotation marks around the words "tooth fairy" that she didn't believe in her anymore. I'm fairly confident that she had begun to doubt even before the tooth fairy failed her, but there was perhaps one last vestige of trust, a glitter-encrusted faith in the mythologies of childhood. That was gone now. I had allowed it to slip through the cracks.

Later, I tried to salvage the experience with a kind of Passover Seder afikomen hunt. I hid the tooth, she found it, and sold it to me for thirteen dollars. It was okay, though there was something vaguely reminiscent of a cash transaction about the whole thing. Not a whole lot of magic.

Sophie had thirteen years of the tooth fairy, I told myself, a good long run. Still, it was a sign that my attentions are divided enough. It's a sign that juggling the needs, desires, fears, wants, and teeth of four children is both joyful and difficult enough for me, without complicating matters with a fifth.

So this is it. Four wonderful children. More children than I ever thought I'd have, certainly. A big family. The perfect size for us. And yet, remember the eggshell toenails and buttery soft skin of a baby's foot? Just one more tiny mouthful of a foot . . .

17. The Audacity of Hope

For the last few years a video has been working its way around the Internet. You know how these things go, for months no one notices them, and then suddenly thirty people send you the link on the same day. I'd watched the video before, a few times, I think, and thought it was cute and a little bit silly. It made me smile.

For four minutes and twenty-eight seconds, some guy named Matt (Matthew Harding, a thirty-something white man from Connecticut living out a protracted and very sweet adolescence) dances the same goofy dance in dozens of different countries. At first he's dancing alone, in an alley in Mumbai, on a hillside in Paro, Bhutan, atop a causeway in Northern Ireland. But soon people start to join in, a group of small children in Antsiranana, Madagascar, a bunch of hipsters in Stockholm, kids in school uniforms in the Solomon Islands, a blank-faced soldier in the demilitarized zone in Korea, a troupe of dancers in candy-colored saris in Gurgaon, India, Papua New Guineans in feathers and paint, a beluga whale in Vava'u, Tonga. The music, by the composer Garry Schyman, has one of those incredible melodies that clicks into your limbic system like a key into a lock, releasing a wash of serotonin or dopamine or something that makes you happy to be alive. It was in Madrid, when a crowd of joyful people rushed out from both sides of the screen, gyrating wildly, a giddy swirl of *alegría*, that I started to cry. I kept it up through Chakachino and Cape of

Good Hope, Timbuktu and Tokyo, San Francisco and São Paulo, and didn't stop until Matt did, in Seattle.

I was crying at the sight of this chubby American dude, a self-described deadbeat with no plan other than to travel the world until his cash ran out, kicking up his heels and swinging his arms atop mountains and temples, in alleyways and on beaches, because Matt's world, where strangers gleefully join you in your dance, is the world that I have always told my children we live in.

For all that I profess such a wholehearted belief in honesty, I have been committing that worst of maternal crimes on a near-daily basis. I have been lying to my children. I've been feeding them this tale about how if they came across a Bedouin in the Negev desert, he would welcome them into his tent and serve them a cup of mint tea, and that if they found themselves in Burkina Faso, a seven-year-old kid might kick around a soccer ball with them, and when lost on the Métro, they are likely to be given directions to the Musée d'Orsay by a haughty but polite Parisian matron with a bichon frise tucked under her arm.

It's not that I would not warn them, say, that while on the Via Veneto in Rome it's wise to clamp a hand over their wallets if rushed by a group of Gypsy kids, or that I would allow them to apply to a student exchange program in Harare, Zimbabwe. I'm not sheltering them from the truth, exactly. The older ones know what an IED is, and that hundreds of thousands of people, both soldiers and civilians, have been killed and maimed in Iraq. They know what happened in Abu Ghraib. All four kids are conversant in the looming global-warming crisis (when she finds a light on, Rosie is apt to snap it off and shout, "Are you people *trying* to kill the polar bears?") and they hate John McCain with a passion they normally reserve for . . . well . . . Dick Cheney. They know it would probably not be safe for our family to travel to certain countries because my passport lists my birthplace as Jerusalem, and they worried about their friends who were lucky enough to go to China for the Olympics because the air pollution in Beijing is, Zeke tells me, some of the worst in the world.

They are not naive children. But in a way they are *innocent*. As honest as I've been about all the world's calamities, I've also tried, despite knowing full well that I was deceiving them, to instill in my kids a faith that at heart all people are just like them, and that justice, if it is not prevailing now, is bound to one day.

That woman who told me when Zeke was a baby that I was imposing my negative view of the universe on my children had it only half-right. On the one hand, I've successfully managed to raise at least one punk rock kid, Zeke, who periodically becomes convinced that the human race has, on balance, brought little but destruction to the world, and that it would be best if our species, like the saber-toothed tiger or the great auk, simply became extinct. But at the same time I've also so successfully sugarcoated the world that Zeke is able to have his faith in human decency completely restored just by listening to Rush ("And the men who hold high places, must be the ones to start, to mold a new reality, closer to the heart"). Which is worse? Lying about hope or telling the truth about hopelessness?

The myth Michael and I have been telling our kids—that each individual in the world shares a core of human decency—has a corollary in the way we discuss the history of America. Our kids get a slightly more honest view of American history than we did back in the 1970s, but the lessons being taught today are not that different in tone from those bygone rose-colored paeans to melting pot and opportunity. While our children learn in school that Columbus cannot be said to have discovered America, they are also told that he did make a very important journey. As the song they teach Berkeley schoolchildren every Indigenous Peoples Day goes, "It was a courageous thing to do, but someone was already here, yes, someone was already here." Because their teachers wouldn't, Michael and I taught them (with the assistance of the brilliant Sarah Vowell and Ira Glass's *This American Life*) about the Trail of Tears, and the brutality of Andrew Jackson, but we also told them about heroes like Tecumseh and Sitting Bull. We wanted to make sure that while they understand this country's history of brutality, they also saw grace and courage. We taught them that once, in the far past, women were not allowed to vote, but now, thanks to suffragists like Susan B. Anthony and Elizabeth Cady Stanton, Hillary Clinton can run for president and California can be represented in the Senate by not one but two women.

You see where I'm going here? We teach them about our nation's history of racism—I once played the older kids Billie Holiday's "Strange Fruit," and we talked about how lynchings were common not so long ago in the South—but then we tell them that thanks to people like Martin Luther King Jr. and Rosa Parks, whom Sophie portrayed in her nursery school's civil rights pageant, the struggle for civil rights was won. (I think Ms. Parks might have enjoyed the sight of a little white moppet furiously refusing to sit at the back of a cardboard-box bus.) My kids are proud to live in the Bay Area, where there is a mayor like Gavin Newsom, brave enough to stand up for justice and allow gay people to marry. We spend a lot of time talking about injustice in our family, but the way we tell it, those days are mostly over. The Voting Rights Act passed into law, and equal protection means that every individual, regardless of race, ethnicity, nationality, or sexual orientation, is entitled to be treated the same. We tell them that the end of racism and prejudice of all kinds is inevitable. I spout to my children an optimistic version of America and the world, in which bad things happen but good people of all kinds struggle for and ultimately receive justice. But I have always feared, in my heart of hearts, that I have been selling them a bill of goods.

Michael is a natural patriot. If it were up to him, we'd have an American flag flying from a pole in front of our house, not because he is naive about what the flag has come to mean both here and abroad, but because he refuses to allow jingoistic bigots who substitute a flag pin for a commitment to the Constitution to own that symbol of freedom. I'm the one who won't have it. *Freedom?* I scoff. To a kid on the streets of Iraq or Iran, of Kigali or Rafah, the American flag sure as hell doesn't symbolize freedom.

But it *should*, Michael says. And if we keep up the struggle, if we don't cede the nation to people and parties whose conception of liberty begins and ends with the right to keep a loaded semi-automatic pistol tucked into the waistband of their jeans, if we keep teaching our children that America is a fundamentally decent place, the flag will one day be a symbol that we can take pride in.

What comes easy to him had to be learned by me. When he tells those stories to our children, a large enough part of him believes what he's saying. But I was raised by Canadian parents whose defining attitude toward the United States was a distrust of its power and rhetoric. My father, who after thirty years in New Jersey finally became a citizen solely so he could vote against George Bush, always wanted to move back to Israel. He and my mother, who was born in Brooklyn but grew up in Montreal, taught me that while the United States was a fine enough place to live, its citizens were in many ways as foreign to us as Masai warriors or Ladakhi sheepherders. My parents instilled in their children not just a suspicion of the U.S. government but a sense of superiority toward its citizens, at least those that didn't live in New York or teach at a select few institutions of higher learning. Americans were stupid, bovine, easily fooled by conniving politicians and telemarketers. They watched hours of television every day. (As did we, but that didn't keep us from looking down our noses. We watched *Masterpiece Theatre* and M*A*S*H, they watched soap operas and game shows.)

The stories we tell our kids come easier to Michael in part because, unlike me, he spent his childhood in a place that inspired patriotism. He grew up in Columbia, Maryland, in the 1970s, when that planned community came close to achieving its utopian ideal of racial integration. In Columbia black and white families lived side by side. White and black children rode their bikes together along the meandering paths, swam together in the neighborhood pools, got into arguments, made up. They were *friends*.

Even if I were not already predisposed to feel both alien and superior to the country in which I spent the vast majority of my life, my hometown wasn't anything to be proud of, particularly when it came to race. I grew up in Ridgewood, New Jersey, a town where real estate agents routinely steered minority families to certain neighborhoods. The African American kids were isolated, segregated, and we white kids made little or no attempt to cross over that divide.

As a little girl, I knew there was a problem, but it never occurred to me that I could do anything about it. It was just another reason to hate my hometown. Now, as an adult, I am not only conscious of and ashamed of my failure to act, but I'm also damaged by it. When Michael meets someone of another race, he does not pretend to be color-blind, or to deny the omnipresence of race, but neither does he bring with him any expectations or biases. But because I did not spend my life in the company of a diversity of people, I'm not as comfortable as he is. I am so conscious of the historical context of oppression in which my conversations take place that sometimes I end up making a fool of myself, trotting out my liberal credentials to prove that I'm one of the good guys.

But part of the story we're teaching our own children is that things like that don't happen anymore. America is different. And it's not entirely a lie. *Their* America *is* different. Berkeley isn't Ridgewood, or Indiana, or even Columbia. They go to schools that not only celebrate diversity but actually embody it. One of Zeke's best friends is a kid whose parents between the two of them encompass four ethnic identities: Jewish, Greek, African American, and white. His other buddy came to Oakland as a refugee from Mississippi after Katrina. Together the three of them look like a Benetton ad.

In my children's world the girl adopted from China by two Jewish lesbians is no more unusual than the kid whose parents hail from the Iowa cornfields. Less, probably. In the year 2000, the first in which the census permitted people to check a box to describe themselves as mixed-race, nearly 5 percent of Californians chose that option. One in nineteen children in the United States is of mixed race, and in California that number is closer to one in ten.

Things *do* look better for my children, and perhaps because of that I have very recently started to wonder if the tales we've been teaching them about the victory of the civil rights movement and the power of diversity might not be the truth, after all.

Not long ago, I was reading the *New York Times*, and was stopped short by a full-page ad for an exclusive real estate agency— a photograph of a family in their lavish, high-ceilinged kitchen, complete with Sub-Zero fridge, expensive wood paneling, and a European cappuccino maker. What was striking about the ad was not that the man and woman were far too young, thin, and fresh faced to really be the parents of the four gorgeous children, but that the "father" was white and the "mother" was black. The family being used to sell a vision of American achievement and luxury was biracial.

I was in Columbia, South Carolina, during the Democratic primary, volunteering for Barack Obama. The night of the election I was standing in a crowd of hundreds waiting for our candidate to take the stage. While they waited, people amused themselves by watching the news on the JumboTron, batting beach balls over their heads, and taking up various chants.

Bill Clinton's face appeared five feet tall on the television screen, a replay of his now-notorious reference to Jesse Jackson having also won the South Carolina primary, with its implication that this year's black candidate's victory would be as fleeting and ultimately irrelevant. In response, a group of black college students took up the chant "Race doesn't matter, race doesn't matter." Within moments the cry spread throughout the room.

There we were, a crowd divided roughly in half between white people and people of color, most of whom were black, in a city where the Confederate flag still flies and where there still stands a statue of Governor Benjamin Tillman, famous for boasting of his murder of blacks who dared to vote: "We shot them. We are not ashamed of it." And we were all shouting, "Race doesn't matter."

Now, of course, race matters. America is still a country where nearly a quarter of African Americans live in poverty and more African American men are in prison than in college. Sixteen years ago, when I was living in Cambridge, Massachusetts, and dating a black fellow law student, race sure as hell mattered. Even in the birthplace of the abolitionist movement people stared at us. Cabs refused to pick us up. People avoided sitting next to us in movie theaters or on the bus.

But now there's that ad in the paper. There are those students in the crowd. There is Barack Obama himself, who doesn't so much espouse the rhetoric of equality and the end of racism as embody it. And there's Matt, boogying down in Amman and in Tel Aviv. And there is the evidence of my four white children, who count among their friends children of any number of races and permutations of racial identity. My kids no longer see the world in black and white. The other day Abe was describing two people. One, he said, was bald, with pink skin. The other wore a red shirt and had black hair and brown skin. Skin was something that could be described by color, like hair, but that's all it was. No race, no politics. Just color.

I'm not naive. I know that soon enough Abe will learn how racial differences and distinctions continue to preoccupy American society. But he's growing up in a world where an advertiser's ideal family is multihued, and where young people can lead a chant that embodies not only the feeling of a moment but the hope for our country's future.

He and his siblings are growing up in the America of our stories, and I can't quite believe it. Maybe all along, like a Good Mother, I've been telling the truth about that good country, America. And maybe it's time for us to get that Stars and Stripes, after all.

18. The Life I Want for Them

At every parents' night I've ever attended—and with four children I've been to more than my share—I have waited for the inevitable question. After we have studied the self-portraits and birthday charts that decorate the walls, after we've signed up (or not) to chaperone the field trips, after the teacher has presented the year's curriculum and the parent-teacher conference schedule, one of the parents always raises his or her hand, a little too high and a little too eagerly.

"What accommodation," he or she says, "do you make for the exceptionally gifted child?"

All the other parents look to find out who the lucky speaker is; who is the parent of this future Bobby Fischer, this Stephen Hawking of the second grade?

For the vast majority of us, the question serves only to make us feel bad. We've all wished at one time or another to be the parents of the gifted kid. Our kitchen drawers are brimming over with abandoned flash cards, Baby Einstein DVDs gather dust in our television cabinets, and our children's toy chests are littered at their lowest levels with the polygon rubble of black-and-white-striped Stim Mobiles, mini baseball gloves, and broken violin bows. I should know. Michael and I still swear to this day that Sophie said the word "duck" when she was only six months old.

It was Sophie who began for us what became a long lesson in the folly of expectations. When she was in preschool, I began buying her First Readers, convinced that it was only a matter of months before she'd be whipping through *The Chronicles of Narnia*. When she was still painstakingly sounding out words at age seven, I called my mother, completely distraught. "She's only reading at a first-grade level!" I wailed.

There was silence on the other end of the line.

Finally my mother said, "Honey, she's *in* first grade."

More hysteria. "But Michael was reading by age four! And I was such an early reader!"

"What are you talking about?" my mother said. "You took forever to learn to read. You were the last in your class."

What?

Still, even knowing of my own average kindergarten abilities didn't prevent me from being disappointed that my daughter didn't excel. Why is it no longer enough for us that our children do well? They must, instead, be prodigies. Top of the class doesn't cut it. They have to be taken from the class and enrolled in a special program for future Nobel laureates.

When Sophie was five years old, she began playing the violin. Or, rather, I *made* her begin playing the violin. It was because of Max. Max was a boy Michael's brother used to babysit for, a boy who, at Sophie's age, played angelic Bach cantatas on a quarter-sized cello. I was sure, or rather I surely hoped, that Sophie had a natural ear, and she looked so cute with her quarter-sized violin.

By the time of her uncle's wedding, Sophie had been studying nearly a year, the last month of which was spent preparing a Russian dance from her Suzuki violin book.

Sophie mounted the stage in her lavender taffeta-and-tulle gown, a circlet of roses in her hair (her first duty of the day had been as flower girl). The crowd hushed as she lifted her violin into position and raised her bow. Every guest in the audience sat a little straighter, wondering just how stunning the prodigy would be when she launched into her flawless Mozart minuet, or perhaps one of Paganini's more simple Capriccios. I knew better, of course, and yet when her bow hit the strings, I sat with my heart in my mouth, full of pride and expectation. You see, my capacity for expectation was forever distorted by Hollywood and that rotten little Max, and part of me was sure that her rendition of this little Russian dance would be the most beautiful, transporting performance of that supremely minor bit of violin music that any of us would ever have heard. This even though I had been listening to her for months; I knew that Sophie playing the violin sounded exactly like a violin rolling itself halfheartedly down the stairs. I knew that her clearest note was in the same exact pitch as my teakettle. After all, I was the one who kept rushing into the kitchen during her lessons to turn off the unlit burner. And yet when the performance began, and the cats in the neighborhood yowled back, recognizing her squall, I was as shocked as anyone in that audience.

The pictures came out great, though! Sophie looks adorable, her curls bouncing beneath their crown of flowers. For all you can tell, she might be playing the allemande from Bach's Partita no. 2 for solo violin.

Why is it that when our children fail to meet our unrealistically high expectations—when they behave, instead, like normal, average kids—we end up disappointed? We send them to after-school cram programs that have terrorized generations of Japanese schoolchildren into higher test scores and mental collapse, we hire pitching coaches and gymnastics tutors, we enroll them in chess camp.

We contemporary parents are convinced, just like the fictional population of Lake Wobegon, Minnesota, that all of our children are above average. But here's the thing: intelligence, like most accomplishment, is a bell curve. There's a large group in the middle, and only a very few outliers on either end. Thus, most of our children rest comfortably in the fat part of that curve. The only thing worse than having low expectations of your children is setting the bar so high that they cannot hope to succeed. And the only thing worse than that is allowing yourself to be crushed when they fail. I know; I've been there. I have seen what happens when the children of whom you have such unrealistically high expectations not only don't excel, but lag behind.

After his horrible year in fourth grade, when we sent Zeke to be evaluated, I think I expected the neuropsychologist to say something like "This child is so brilliant and sophisticated that sometimes his frustration with the low level of work in the classroom makes him act out." I can hear you laughing. At least those of you whose children have gone through the rigamarole of testing and diagnosis. I'll bet there are others who are thinking, "That sounds about right. Poor Dylan/Parker/Jayden/Storey is just not getting the stimulation he needs."

I went into the meeting confident that my child's genius would be confirmed. This was the boy, after all, who could recite the planets in order from the sun when he was fifteen months old. Of course he could also recite the names of TV's Arthur and all his classmates, and there didn't actually seem to be much of a difference in how he'd learned both. He's got a great *long-term* memory. The last thing I was expecting was a diagnosis of ADHD and of the other series of challenges my older son faces. The doctor spent over two hours with us that morning, going over every page of his thick pile of test results. I started crying almost immediately, something fairly typical, I suppose, if the boxes of tissues placed strategically around the office were anything to gauge by.

When I recall it now, it was almost as though, in the days and weeks that followed, I went through a version of Kübler-Ross's stages of grief. First came denial. There was nothing wrong with my son, I insisted. To a hammer, everything looks like a nail, and to a neuropsychologist every behavior looks like a learning disability. The tests were wrong, administered poorly, graded incorrectly. My boy wasn't hyperactive; he didn't run frantically from place to place, jumping off furniture and breaking dishes. He didn't have attention problems; he could sit for two hours perfecting a Flair-pen drawing of Mothra battling Godzilla. Zeke was fine, the problem was school. His teachers didn't understand him; they couldn't see past his (admittedly crappy) attitude to the sensitive brilliance that lay beneath. Moreover, the whole academic enterprise was structured for girls, not for boys. Show me any ten-year-old boy who could sit still for an hour multiplying decimals. It can't be true, I said. ADHD is one of those fad diagnoses, a way to pathologize the behavior of normal boys. The medical and educational establishment wants to drug our children into dull compliance.

Although I've moved beyond the stage of denial, I still think there was some truth to my initial flood of defensiveness. Schools are organized to cater to more sedentary, well-behaved children, to the kinds of kids who can concentrate for hours at a time, even without periodic recess breaks spent crashing madly around a playground. It was also true that Zeke is not hyperactive in the way that laymen think of the disorder; you rarely see him bouncing off the walls.

But even as I was ranting and remonstrating, I knew that I was being unreasonable. While he might not tear a room apart (he's a neat boy), Zeke does have "impulse control" issues. That phrase rang true the moment the neuropsychologist first uttered it. I thought of the impulses Zeke had failed to control: the impulse to use his new pocketknife to shred the seat of his desk chair and the upholstery in the back of the minivan (how does one balance the cost of having to replace leather car upholstery against the pleasure of being able to say to one's husband, "I told you a knife was no gift for a child"?); the impulse to tackle a mean kid who was teasing him; the impulse to knock down his younger siblings' elaborate "setup" (a family term that means a panorama made of small toys, like Playmobils or Legos, or the beloved Hamtaros, tiny plastic hamsters based on the Japanese anime TV series).

The diagnosis of processing-speed delay made sense, too. This was why Zeke was always slow at figuring out the value of his Yahtzee roll. I felt so ashamed of all the times I had berated him, saying something like, "Come *on*, Zeke, you *know* what three times three is." And of course he did. It just took him an extra fraction of a second to come up with the answer. It was a miracle that he could do it at all, with me hollering in his ear.

The next phase I went through was a kind of collapse, in which I actually stopped *seeing* my son, the boy whom I know better, in many ways, than I know myself. I forgot everything I knew about who he was and what he was capable of, and began to panic that he would become lost in the world. The possibilities for his future, which I had once seen as boundless, suddenly seemed constricted and limited. He would not, as I had promised him since he was a baby, be able to do anything and be anything, with only the limitations of his imagination to constrain him. There were skills that would forever be beyond him, jobs he would never be fit to assume. It was in the throes of this bitter phase that I said to Michael, "If he's got processing-speed problems, he'll never be able to be an airline pilot!"

Doing his best not to smile, Michael said, "I don't think he's ever wanted to be an airline pilot."

"I know that! But if he ever wants to, he won't be able to."

"He won't be able to play in the NBA, either," Michael said. "That's never bothered you."

Indeed I had never lost a moment's sleep over the fact that my son would never be a professional basketball player, or a professional athlete of any kind. Michael's right—I've never cared one whit about my children's athletic limitations. On the contrary, I brag as much about the time Zeke kicked a ball into the opposing team's soccer goal as other parents brag about their children's amateur tennis rankings.

But to have my child be limited by something in his *brain*: that thought tortured me. Now, a year later, picking apart my reaction, I can see that this period of panic and fear had two distinct elements. I was afraid for my son, for how hard he would have to struggle to do well in school, for the ways in which he might not be able to do all he wanted, or achieve all his dreams. But there was also a much more shameful element. One that even now I can hardly bear to admit. I was afraid for him, but I was also *disappointed*. I was crushed at least in part because of my own ego. Part of me wanted to be, had always wanted to be, the one with the hand in the air. "What accommodation," I was afraid I would now never be able to say, "will you make for my gifted child?"

I had these expectations, you see, born of my own and Michael's academic successes, that our children would be not just smart but smart*er*. I had met all these exceptionally smart children even before I had my own, like the son of college friends who at age four could warble long bits of opera—in *Italian*. The ten-year-old son of people we know works weekends as a sous chef at one of the Bay Area's finest restaurants. Other people's children made their debuts with the Berlin Philharmonic; they sat in Washington Square Park, the heels of their Stride Rites pounding a tattoo on the bench, as they trounced old Russian grand masters at blitz chess. They did quadratic equations in their heads while they were still in diapers. *That* was what my children were supposed to be like. Even before I had them, I knew they would be brilliant. They would be plucked from their schoolrooms and taken to the gifted class. They would play Mozart at age three. They would shine brighter and do better than any other child. There was no room in my elaborate scaffolding of expectations for something like ADHD.

As much as I loathe to admit it, I was fearful of the reactions of the mothers of those perfect, gifted children. I was embarrassed. And certainly there have been mothers (and fathers) who have justified that concern. I cannot tell you how many people have responded to news of Zeke's diagnosis with disapproving versions of my own initial reaction, informing me of the dangers of over-medicating. They've said, "Boys will be boys." They've raised their eyebrows; they've been smug or pitying. But just as often, people have responded to my (or Zeke's) admission with the whispered confession that their son needs medication, too, or their daughter is learning disabled, or can I please, *please*, give them a referral to Zeke's therapist.

The thing is, you can never really know what goes on behind the closed doors of other houses, and what seems like brilliance and feels like superiority almost always has its own quota of trouble. Things are rarely ever what they seem. That math genius? He was still taking a nightly bottle when he was seven. The opera singer is dyslexic. And while the infant chess master is indeed brilliant, he's also a narcissistic little pill.

On Zeke's first day of summer day camp this year he came home in a gloom. Everyone knew each other, he told us. They all went to school together. They had secret handshakes, in-jokes, private nicknames. They knew whom to sit with, and just what to say. And there he was, on the outs. He would never make a friend.

As parents, we had the presence of mind and the experience to tell him that the way things feel from the outside is rarely the truth of the matter. The people at the fantastic party you think you didn't get invited to don't even know there's a party going on. They don't feel any more a part of the brilliance than you do. We have a tendency to value idealization over our own experience of messy reality. We fail to recognize that reality is actually wonderful, but for reasons that have absolutely nothing to do with the ideal.

The reality of Zeke perhaps did not live up to some fantastically ludicrous ideal of a child I had in my head, the perfect counterpart to the ideal of the Good Mother I dreamed and despaired of being, but what I finally realized, when I passed out of that ugly and painful stage of grief, was that nothing about my son had changed. The neuropsychologist's diagnosis had not infected Zeke with a disease. It was nothing more than a description of a small part of who he was, who he'd always been. And he was still exactly the same person. He was still the same little boy who'd named all the planets, still the same politically savvy kid who cracked jokes about Donna Brazile, still the same boy who picked up his little sister at ballet class and walked her home, gripping her chubby little paw in one of his hands and her tiny pink slippers in the other. Zeke is exactly what he's always been, creative and very intelligent, with a heightened awareness of injustice and a mordant wit. He is the little toddler who held my cheeks in his hands, gazed into my eyes, and said with utmost seriousness and certitude, "Mommy, I love you." What I love about my boy is unlabelable. Who he is can never be quantified by pages of test scores, no matter the size of the sheaf.

The whole notion of the constriction of potential that I had cried over so hard, I see, is just absurd. True, you wouldn't want to fly in a plane piloted by Zeke, nor will he ever solve the Goldbach conjecture. But as Michael said, he's never had aviation aspirations, and he's doing fine in math. The point of a life, any life, is to figure out what you are good at, and what makes you happy, and, if you are very fortunate, spend your life doing those things.

What the diagnosis gave us was a way to help our son. He now has, in the jargon of his various tutors and therapists, a full toolbox of techniques with which to do well in school. He is learning math through a teaching program designed for brains like his, and doing well.* He has an ed therapist to help him figure out how to approach his homework. And on school days—only on school days—he takes Ritalin, which allows him to ignore the distractions around him and concentrate on his teacher and his work and on controlling his impulses.

The worst thing about being so devoted to your expectations is that it blinds you to the wonders of the children you have. When Rosie was little, she was a slow talker. At the age at which her siblings were discoursing in long, complicated sentences, she was just beginning to put words together in non-syntactical combinations. She spoke in the most adorable baby talk, but much of the time when I should have been enjoying her babble and celebrating her new words, I was distracted by the nagging worry that she was behind the curve. She would sit on the floor, her fat legs stretched out in front of her, as I built and rebuilt a tower of blocks, laughing each time I toppled it over. I was so busy saying, "Rosie, can you say 'boom'? Say 'boom' for Mommy," that I barely

*The program's called Making Math Real. It's incredible. Sitting in the room during one of his sessions, I learned my six times table for the first time in my life.

205

registered her full-body smile, the way every inch of her, from her cornflower blue eyes to the pink tips of her toes, wriggled as she grinned at the tower's collapse.

The most toxic thing parents can do is allow their delight and pride in their children to be spoiled by disappointment, by frustration when the children fail to live up to expectations formed before they were even born, expectations that have nothing to do with them and everything to do with the parents' own egos.

One of my favorite yoga teachers, the one I go to because she works me the hardest and makes me the skinniest, spends a lot of the time we are inhaling through alternate nostrils talking about right mindfulness, the Buddhist notion of bringing awareness to the present moment, of consciously shifting our attention away from the past and the future and focusing it on the present, on the moment, on the instant at hand. To be mindful means you do not judge or evaluate, you simply experience. Notice. Concentrate on the moment, be aware of it as it happens without stopping to try to figure out what it means.

It feels ridiculous even to write about this, about Buddhism and yoga. I do not meditate, although I know I should and I have periodically tried. The voices in my head are as multitudinous and persistent as the lice that infest my children's hair at the beginning of every school year. Moreover, I actually kind of hate people who talk about things like mindfulness, or at least the ones I run into around here, in Berkeley. Why is it that the most self-actualized people seem so often to be the most self-absorbed?

I'm no Buddhist, but still I wish I were a more mindful mother. A mindful mother would not get so knotted up about breast-feeding that she would forget that her job was simply to love her baby and keep him healthy, without torturing herself and him with that infernal pump. A mindful mother would not be so worried about her children being bipolar that she would be too afraid to laugh when her daughter reported hearing a voice in her head. It was not the fact of the voice that was funny (although neither, really, was it a cause for alarm). It was whose voice it was, and what it was saying. At the height of the 2008 Democratic primary, six-year-old Rosie awoke in the middle of the night wailing, "I can't get the voice out of my head!"

"What voice?" I said, panicking. "What is the voice telling you to do?" Immediately, I saw the rest of our lives. My beautiful fairy daughter, the sparkle in her eyes dimmed by Thorazine, struggling against the straps of her straitjacket, while I stood helplessly by, unable to save her.

Rosie clutched her skull with both hands and whipped her head back and forth. "It's Hillary Clinton!" she wailed. "Health care, health care, health care, she just won't shut up!"

The thing to remember, in our quest to do right by our children and by ourselves, is that while we struggle to conform to an ideal or to achieve a goal, our life is happening around us, without our noticing. If we are too busy or too anxious to pay attention, it will all be gone before we have time to appreciate it.

The irony is, of course, that by thinking about mindfulness, I could just be setting up another unattainable goal, another way to fail at this impossible of jobs. A Good Mother is a mindful mother. A distracted mother, what is she? Surely you know by now: a Bad Mother.

But still, perhaps it's worth the risk.

Even if I'm setting myself up for failure, I think it's worth trying to be a mother who delights in who her children are, in their knock-knock jokes and earnest questions. A mother who spends less time obsessing about what will happen, or what has happened, and more time reveling in what *is*. A mother who doesn't fret over failings and slights, who realizes that her worries and anxieties are just thoughts, the continuous chattering and judgment of a too busy mind. A mother who doesn't worry so much about being bad or good, but just recognizes that she's both, and neither. A mother who does her best, and for whom that is good enough, even if, in the end, her best turns out to be, simply, not bad.

Acknowledgments

With profound gratitude to the Mesa Refuge in Point Reyes, California.

To Mary Evans.

To Meredith Maran, Peggy Orenstein, Sylvia Brownrigg, Nancy Johnson, Peter Barnes, Daniel Handler (whose idea this was in the first place), Cheri Hickman, and Sharon Chabon.

To Kate Moses, Camille Peri, Emily Nussbaum, Lauren Kern, Daniel Jones, Lori Leibovich, Gary Kamiya, Tom Dolby, Melissa de la Cruz, and Ilena Silverman.

To Carmen Dario, Xiomara Batin, Megan Cody, Erin Gepner, and Simone Cohen.

To Phyllis Grann, Jackeline Montalvo, Alison Rich, Julie Sills, and Steve Rubin.

And especially to my mother, Ricki Waldman, and to my husband, Michael Chabon. They are responsible for what's best in me.

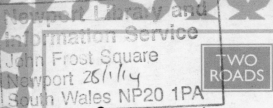

TWO
ROADS

Stories . . . voices . . . places . . . lives

Two Roads is the home of great storytelling and reader
enjoyment. We publish stories from the heart, told in
strong voices about lives lived. Two Roads books come
from everywhere and take you into other worlds.

We hope you enjoyed *Bad Mother*. If you'd like to know
more about this book or any other title on our list,
please go to www.tworoadsbooks.com or scan this code
with your smartphone to go straight to our site:

For news on forthcoming Two Roads titles, please sign up
for our newsletter.

We'd love to hear from you

enquiries@tworoadsbooks.com

 Twitter (@tworoadsbooks)
 facebook.com/TwoRoadsBooks
 pinterest.com/tworoadsbooks